Robes of the Realm

Robes of the Realm

300 Years of Ceremonial Dress

UNA CAMPBELL

FOREWORD BY

H.R.H. THE PRINCE OF WALES

Tercentenary Celebrations in Association with The Prince's Trust

Ede and Ravenscroft LTD

MICHAEL O'MARA BOOKS LIMITED

Designed and produced by
Michael O'Mara Books Limited
for Ede and Ravenscroft Ltd
93 Chancery Lane, London WC2A 1DU

First published in Great Britain by
Michael O'Mara Books Limited
20 Queen Anne Street, London W1N 9FB, 1989

British Library Cataloguing in Publication Data

Campbell, Una
    Robes of the realm: 300 years of ceremonial dress
    1. Great Britain, Ceremonial costume. Ede and
    Ravenscroft Ltd
    I. Title
    338.7'68715'0941

    ISBN 0-948397-61-6

Editor: Serena Dilnot
Design: Simon Bell

Distributed to the UK book trade by
Michael O'Mara Books Limited

Typeset by Florencetype Ltd, Kewstoke, Avon
Origination by Fotographics Ltd, London and Hong Kong
Printed and bound in Spain by Graficas Estella S.A.

Frontispiece *A customer is fitted for a court suit*

Contents

I am delighted that my Trust will benefit from the sales of Ede and Ravenscroft's *Robes of the Realm* which is published to mark their 300 years service to state, church and to the legal profession.

This splendid volume is not only a worthy tribute to their long-standing tradition, but also a valuable addition to the history of British Pageantry. I wish them every success with it.

Charles.

The Ede and Ravenscroft coat of arms

Introduction

Those of us associated with Ede and Ravenscroft are very conscious of Britain's unique heritage of ceremonial custom in which we and our predecessors have been proud to participate over the last three hundred years. This book, produced as part of the firm's Tercentenary celebrations, is our tribute to that heritage, and is dedicated to our workforce, past and present, for the unfailingly high standards of craftsmanship which they have maintained over the years.

We are delighted to be producing this book in association with The Prince's Trust, who will receive the proceeds from its sale. Further information about the Trust and its very valuable work can be obtained from The Administrator at 8 Bedford Row, London WC1R 4BU.

Finally, we would like to acknowledge with gratitude the help that we have received from a great many people in the course of preparing this book for publication. Particular mention should be made of the following: The Rt Hon. Lord Mackay of Clashfern, PC, Lord High Chancellor; The Rt Hon. Bernard Weatherill, PC, MP, Speaker of the House of Commons; Major-General His Grace The Duke of Norfolk, KG, GCVO, CB, CBE, MC, DL, Earl Marshal; The Most Hon. The Marquess of Cholmondeley, GCVO, MC, DL, Lord Great Chamberlain; The Most Hon. The Marquess of Reading; The Rt Hon. The Earl of Shrewsbury and Waterford; The Rt Hon. The Earl of Lichfield; The Rt Hon. The Lord Mayor of London, Sir Christopher Collett, GBE; The Rt Hon. The Viscount Torrington; The Rt Hon. The Lord Stafford; The Rt Hon. Lord Denning, PC, DL; The Rt Hon. The Lord Lane, AFC, Lord Chief Justice; The Rt Hon. The Lord McFadzean, KT; The Rt. Hon. Lord Justice Mann; The Hon. Mr Justice Drake, DFC; General Sir John Hackett, GCB, CBE, DSO, MC, DL; Sir Nicholas Henderson, GCMG; Lieutenant-Colonel Sir Martin Gilliatt, GCVO, MBE; Air Chief Marshal Sir John Gingell, GBE, KCB; His Honour Judge Murchie; The College of Arms, particularly Thomas Woodcock Esq., Somerset Herald of Arms; Albert Batteson Esq.; Graham Heddle Esq.

Michael W. Middleton
Chairman – Ede and Ravenscroft Ltd.

Ede and Ravenscroft

The premises of Ede and Ravenscroft, robemakers of Chancery Lane, are delightfully old-fashioned. The high counter with its mahogany panelling and brass rail has changed little in over a century, and carved mahogany arches link the glazed partitions dividing the interior.

Glass showcases contain a display of mementoes such as Lord Erskine's wig, unworn since the day in the early 19th century when he had the misfortune to drop it into a well famed for its petrifying qualities; indeed, the wig does now appear to be made of stone. In another case are two sets of metal dies used to stamp out black sealskin spots for peers' robes worn at the coronations of George VI and Elizabeth II. Close by are samples of the rich velvets and satins used in robemaking for various coronations, as well as examples from robes worn at the investiture of the Prince of Wales at Caernarvon in 1969.

opposite: The Bar Room, where members of the bar and bench used to have their hair trimmed before their new wigs were fitted. Similar black and gold gowns are worn by high-ranking legal officers, among others.

Ede and Ravenscroft have traded from these premises in Chancery Lane since 1868.

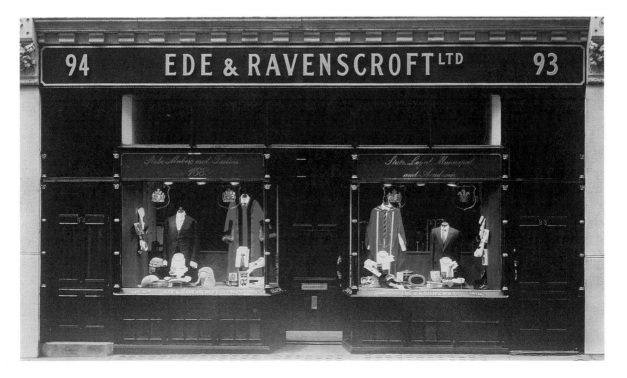

HIS Indenture witnesseth, That _Joseph Eade Son of Joseph Eade of Finsbury Passage Finsbury Square in the County of Middlesex Carpenter_ being paid or secured to the Master as the Consideration for taking his said Apprentice, doth put himself Apprentice to _William Webb Robe Maker_ Citizen and MERCHANT TAYLOR of London, to learn his Art, and with him (after the Manner of an Apprentice) to serve from the Date hereof, until the full End and Term of _Seven_ Years, from thence next following, to be fully complete and ended. During which Term, the said Apprentice his said Master faithfully shall serve, his Secrets keep; his lawful Commandments every where gladly do. He shall do no Damage to his said Master, nor see it to be done of others, but that he, to his Power, shall let, or forthwith give Warning to his said Master of the same. He shall not waste the Goods of his said Master, nor lend them unlawfully to any. He shall not commit Fornication, nor contract Matrimony within the said Term. He shall not play at Cards, Dice, Tables, or any other unlawful Games, whereby his said Master may have any Loss. With his own Goods or others, during the said Term, without Licence of his said Master, he shall neither buy nor sell. He shall not haunt Taverns or Play-houses, nor absent himself from his said Master's Service Day nor Night unlawfully: But in all Things, as a faithful Apprentice, he shall behave himself towards his said Master, and all his, during the said Term. And the said Master his said Apprentice, in the same art which he useth, by the best Means that he can, shall teach and instruct, or cause to be taught and instructed, finding unto his said Apprentice, Meat, Drink, Apparel, Lodging, and all other Necessaries, according to the Custom of the City of London, during the said Term. And for the true Performance of all and every the said Covenants and Agreements, either of the said Parties bind themselves unto the other by these Presents, In witness whereof the Parties above-named to these Indentures interchangeable have put their Hands and Seals, the _fifth_ Day of _June_ in the _Fifty first_ Year of the Reign of our Sovereign Lord GEORGE the _Third_ of the United Kingdom of Great Britain and Ireland, King, and so forth, and in the Year of our Lord, 1811.

The Indenture, Covenant, Article, or Contract must bear Date the Day it is executed; and what Money or other Thing is given or contracted for with the Clerk or Apprentice, must be inserted in Words at Length; and the Duty paid at the Stamp-Office, if in London, or within the Weekly Bills of Mortality, within One Month after the Execution, and if in the Country, and out of the said Bills of Mortality, within Two Months, to a Distributor of Stamps, or his Substitute; otherwise the Indenture will be void, the Master or Mistress forfeit Fifty Pounds, and another Penalty, and the Apprentice be disabled to follow his Trade, or be made free.

Joseph Ede was apprenticed to William Webb in 1811. Twenty-three years later he was running the firm which bears his name to the present day.

On the walls hang a framed letter from the great Lord Nelson concerning his robes as a Knight of the Order of the Bath; the indenture of young Joseph Ede, apprenticed to William Webb in 1811; and, most importantly, a remarkable collection of royal warrants. There are also many paintings and photographs of royal and state dignitaries, resplendent in the ceremonial dress made for them by the firm.

Tucked away behind the scenes is the Bar Room where, during the early part of this century, judges and barristers had their hair trimmed and their new wigs fitted. The room is now used for private meetings, but the two marble shelves with their long mirrors where the barbers worked are still in place and the walls carry an impressive array of small prints, each one depicting the bewigged figure of a judge of yesteryear. Humphrey Ravenscroft patented his own forensic wig in 1822 and Ede and Ravenscroft still make the three types of legal wig – full-bottomed, bench and bar – to his incomparable design.

Amidst all this are the robes: robes awaiting repairs and alterations, fitting or collection; robes in great variety from the deep blue and green velvets of the Orders of the Garter and the Thistle, to the vivid scarlet wool and white miniver fur worn by peers on ceremonial occasions in the House of Lords. The dark shades of academic gowns contrast with a seemingly endless variety of coloured hoods, and with the striking patterns and colours of robes for foreign universities and civic dignitaries.

Over the centuries the firm has supplied robes and wigs to royalty and peers, high court judges and university chancellors, knights and heralds, lord mayors, masters of livery companies, newly qualified barristers and solicitors, and university graduates. Many people have had occasion to be grateful to the staff for their professional expertise and their extensive knowledge of the sometimes complicated traditions of dress and procedure associated with the ceremonial side of their various estates and professions. During the last three centuries Ede and Ravenscroft has established and maintained a reputation as the acknowledged authority on robemaking in all its aspects, based on meticulous attention to detail together with an uncompromising regard for quality of materials and workmanship.

The interior of the Chancery Lane shop would still be recognisable to many past generations of clients. The gold-painted black boxes on the shelves are used to store legal wigs.

Three Hundred Years of Robemaking

The firm now called Ede and Ravenscroft was founded by the Shudall family towards the end of the 17th century. 1689 is the date traditionally given for its establishment (the year of the coronation of William and Mary), but the Shudalls were not newcomers to the trade and records suggest that various family members had employed their skills as tailors and haberdashers within the City of London for a number of years prior to 1689.

The Shudalls ran their business from premises in Holywell Street, 'near the new church in the Strand', and part of their family history can be traced in the records of this new church, St Clement Danes. Holywell Street lay just west of the City boundary at Temple Bar, an area occupied today by the imposing buildings and busy traffic systems of Aldwych. In the 17th century this was a centre of the tailoring trade, with many individual tradesmen – tailors, mercers, robemakers, furriers, embroiderers and haberdashers – working alongside one another and combining their skills as the need arose.

Here William Shudall and his wife, Martha, worked as robemakers during the mid-18th century, while their clerk sat hour by hour keeping the day book and recording in clear copperplate hand the transactions of the firm. As well as tailoring for individuals and on occasion fulfilling orders for other tradesmen, the firm had many customers who were involved in the Church or the State. Cassocks, gowns and coats were made for numerous members of the clergy in London and the surrounding countryside and in due course orders from further afield began to appear in the day book, with robes being made for the bishops of Bangor, Chichester and Norwich. Robes were made for knights of the Order of the Garter and as the time approached for the annual meeting of the Chapter at Windsor there was a flurry of activity to refurbish robes and provide new ribbons and bows and ostrich feathers. This work often involved William Shudall in a trip to Windsor and it is interesting to note that more than one account on 28 March one year carried the following charge:

William III wearing his coronation robes. Ede and Ravenscroft was established in 1689, the year of the coronation of William and Mary.

Mary II's crimson velvet coronation robe was trimmed and fully lined with ermine.

	£	s	d
To Attendance at Windsor for			
self and Servant	3	3	–
To the Carriage of Trunk to			
Windsor and Back		6	–

The Shudalls and those who succeeded them were good record keepers, leaving to more recent owners of the firm a considerable collection of interesting archives, which are now housed in the safekeeping of the Guildhall Library. The day book is perhaps the most valued item, providing a unique and detailed account of the years 1747–62.

After William Shudall's death in 1757 his widow continued to run the business during a decade of much activity. George II died in 1760, and 1761 was a particularly busy year, with Mrs Shudall undertaking a great deal of robemaking for the coronation of George III.

Soon after this the name of Francis Stone, robemaker, begins to appear in the records. Brief references to Messrs Shudall and Stone indicates the existence of a partnership during the few years prior to Mrs Shudall's retirement in about 1770. Francis Stone may have been an independent tradesman of Holywell Street, or perhaps an earlier employee or foreman of the Shudalls – we can only speculate – but he was to continue to run the business throughout the last quarter of the 18th century.

During that time there was little call for work on coronation robes, since George III remained on the throne for sixty years. However, among much other work, we find Francis Stone

George II's coronation robe and surcoat were made of velvet, trimmed with ermine and gold lace. The robe is fully lined with ermine. He is wearing the collar (or chain) of the Order of the Garter, from which hangs the George.

William Webb's invoices were
works of art in themselves.
This one describes the
coronation robes made for a
baron, Lord Braybrook, in
preparation for the coronation
of George IV.

maintaining the firm's position as robemakers to the knights of
the Order of the Garter. One reference to him in the List of
Declared Accounts of Masters of the Robes seems to echo
William Shudall's entries in the firm's day book some thirty
years previously:

Dec. 15th 1790
To a very rich white Ribbon to Tye the Garter Mantle. Atten-
dance for self and foreman, and Coach hire to and from St.
James's at a Chapter of the Order of the Garter

£0   15   –

Received the 23rd August 1791 the Contents of this Bill.

By the end of the 18th century Francis Stone of Holywell Street
was well established. A comparatively wealthy man, he travel-
led between his family home at Cole Green in Hertfordshire
and his robemaking concerns in London and at Court. No
doubt he gained great personal satisfaction from his appointment as robemaker to His Majesty King George III.

Francis Stone died in the spring of 1797, leaving a well-run
and successful business to his son-in-law, William Webb. Mr
Webb had married Ann Stone at St Clement Danes Church in
November 1791. His original occupation had been as an
upholsterer, but he had apparently entered the profession
of robemaking with enthusiasm. A new royal warrant was
granted to him in 1797:

These are to require you to swear and admit Mr William Webb
into the Place and Quality of Robe-Maker in Ordinary to His
Majesty. To have, hold, exercise and enjoy the said Place
together with all Rights, Profits, Privileges and Advantages
thereunto belonging. And for so doing this shall be your Warrant, Given under my Hand & Seal this 15th Day of March 1797
in the Thirty-Seventh Year of His Majesty's Reign.

Salisbury

Once William Webb had settled into his new position he
designed a new invoice for the firm which he was to run in his
own name for almost thirty-five years. It was an ornate affair,
with many embellishments, in keeping with the fashion of his
time. It is also a very informative document, providing 20th-
century researchers with a succinct and vivid picture of his
clients and their requirements. We are told that William Webb

Makes all Kinds of Robes for Peers, Peeresses & Bishops.
Coronation. Installation. Judges, Serjeants, Clergymen, King's
Council, Barristers and Attorneys, Livery-Gowns and Robes for
any Corporation in Great Britain.

Surplices, Pulpit and Communion Furniture made in the neatest
manner.

The R't Hon'ble Lord Braybrook

To W'm Webb

WILLIAM WEBB
Robe Maker

To his Majesty, THE PRINCE OF WALES, and Royal Family.
Son in Law & Successor to M'r FRAN'S STONE, at his late Residence.
The Parliament and Judge Robes.
N.º 37. Hollywell Street near the New Church Strand,
LONDON.

Makes all kinds of Robes for Peers, Peeresses & Bishops, Coronation, Installation,
Judges, Serjeants, Clergymen, Kings Council, Barristers and Attorneys,
Livery Gowns and Robes for any Corporation in Great Britain.
Surplices, Pulpit & Communion Furniture made in the neatest manner.

1820
July 19 To a Silver Gilt Barons Coronet, turn'd with the
richest Crimson Silk Genoa Velvet, the choicest of
Spott d Ermine, Gold Tassell, Silk Lining &c
A Coronation Mantle & Surcoat of the richest Crim'n
Silk Genoa Velvet, trimm'd with the choicest spot'd
Ermine, lined with rich White Silk &c
A Doublet & Trunk of very rich White Satin, trimm'd
with the richest Gold Brocade Plate Lace & Vandyke
Fringe
A Pair of white China Silk Pantaloons with feet
A Pair of " Cotton Drawers D'o
A Coronation Sword, Scabbard & Belt Covered with
rich Crimson Velvet Best Gilt Mountings &c
A Pair of the best White Kid Gloves trimm'd with
the richest deep Gold fringe - - - -
A Pair of the best W't Kid Shoes
A Pair of Knee & Shoe Crimson Ribbon Rosettes -
A fine Linen Robe & Coronet Case - -
A Cedar Chest for Robes with Patent Lock
Brass Hinges, Handles, Inscription Plate &c   £250..0..0

paid by the hand of Mess'rs Welch'd
& Reade, on Tu'r time Oct'r 1820
Braybrook

It is an impressive catalogue but not inappropriate to the royal robemaker at the head of a business which had already been in existence for over a century.

In 1811 William Webb took on an apprentice by the name of Joseph Ede. His indenture, which is on display at 93 Chancery Lane, must have seemed a daunting commitment to the young man who signed it that day and began his working life in Holywell Street. The apprenticeship was for a term of seven years, during which the apprentice undertook that he would 'not commit Fornication, nor contract Matrimony', nor would he 'haunt Taverns or Play-houses', among other prohibitions. However, Joseph Ede was to prove most successful. In time he became William Webb's foreman and his name features prominently in the firm's affairs in later years.

When William Webb died in the autumn of 1831 his robe-making business passed to his son, Frederick, who was then aged thirty. Frederick Webb continued his father's work, assisted by Joseph Ede, and within a few months received a royal warrant appointing him robemaker to William IV. The warrant, signed by the Duke of Devonshire, was dated 5 December 1831, just three months after the coronation.

We know little of the firm's activities at this time but it seems that William Webb's death was followed by a period of decline. Frederick Webb attempted to remedy the situation and one small piece of paper among the archives tells the story. An undated circular letter written from 193 Fleet Street by Frederick Webb, it is brief and to the point:

> I beg most respectfully to solicit your favors, assuring you that, at all times, your commands shall receive my best attention; and that with respect to materials, the best will always be selected – moderate charges, and workmanship such as must give entire satisfaction.

There is no indication of the response to this appeal nor, indeed, of the cause for Frederick Webb's lack of success. The pencil jottings on the reverse of the letter tell their own story:

Fixtures	£170	19	–	Not paid
Furniture & Stock	314	16	–	
Goodwill	460	0	–	
	£774	16	–	

June 25 1834

The purchaser and new owner of the firm was Thomas Adams, a man of some means who also happened to be Joseph Ede's uncle. The discussion and planning that went on behind the scenes can be imagined: it is unlikely that Joseph Ede could

The Prince Regent, later George IV, wearing the robes of a Knight of the Garter. The Tudor-style underdress is no longer worn.

A baron at George IV's coronation in 1821, robed as described in William Webb's invoice (see page 19). *He is attended by his page.*

THE STANDARD OF S? GEORGE,
borne by a Baron in his Coronation Dress and Robes of Estate,
attended by His Page.

have found the capital necessary to acquire the business but he most certainly possessed all the knowledge and expertise required to run it.

In 1834, three years after William Webb's death, the new name of the firm, Adams & Ede, was displayed over the shop at 193 Fleet Street, premises on the south-west corner of Chancery Lane which William Webb had acquired in 1827. There is no further reference to 37 Holywell Street or to 98 Chancery Lane, which was occupied by William Webb for about twenty years and which may well have been part of the area cleared to make way for an extensive programme of rebuilding: the settlement to the west of Chancery Lane known as the Rookeries, a notorious slum area, was razed to the ground at this time in preparation for the construction of many new buildings including the Royal Courts of Justice facing on to the Strand.

The move from 37 Holywell Street to 193 Fleet Street in 1827 marked the end of an era, for the firm had traded from premises in Holywell Street for over one hundred and thirty-five years. The Poor Rate levied on 37 Holywell Street had been paid annually from 1741 by William Shudall, by his widow Martha, by Francis Stone, and latterly, by William Webb. Prior to 1741 the Shudall family had traded from a house some few doors along Holywell Street and the records confirm their payment of the rates there from before 1689.

On 30 June 1834 Joseph Ede was appointed robemaker to His Majesty King William IV, continuing the firm's unbroken record as holders of royal warrants. Under Joseph Ede's direction business began to increase and during the Victorian era the firm enjoyed a time of growing prosperity. Joseph Ede was appointed robemaker to Her Majesty Queen Victoria on 7 August 1837, shortly after her accession to the throne. It was the first of a series of warrants which the firm was granted throughout Queen Victoria's long reign.

The day book for 1837–8 is of particular interest as a reflection of events of the time. In the days preceding the funeral of William IV the clerk was kept busy recording sales of mourning bands and weepers, part of the legal profession's mourning wear. The bands are similar to the ordinary bands, or linen tabs, worn around the neck, but have a central pleat; weepers are special white handkerchiefs tucked into the wide cuffs of a court coat and turned back over them. Two mourning bands were required for the Registrar's Office; two bands and two pairs of weepers for Sir W.W. Follett; one pair of weepers for J. Wigram Esq.; and for the Lord Chancellor, twelve mourning bands and six pairs of weepers.

By the spring of 1838 preparations for Queen Victoria's coronation were well advanced and the ledgers list accounts for numerous peers of all degrees. Some required new coronation robes and coronets, while others brought robes belonging to their predecessors: these were duly altered or repaired. Coronets, too, were altered to fit their new owners, regilded, lined with new velvet, and given new ermine borders and gold tassels.

The new ledgers from 1835–60 bear witness to a wide range of custom, from single items sold to private individuals to the quarterly accounts rendered to the Lord Chamberlain's Office and to Buckingham Palace. Work undertaken for private individuals can for the most part be separated into four distinct categories, representing members of the legal and academic professions, holders of civic and municipal office, and those of an ecclesiastical calling.

Random examples from Joseph Ede's day books give an insight into the firm's trade in the mid-19th century:

		£	s	d
2 Jan 1836	George Farren Esq. A Bar Gown & 2 Bands	3	9	–
2 Jan 1836	Corporation of Saffron Walden A mayor's gown of fine princes stuff, velvet facings & cape, & silk tufts	145	10	–
21 June 1837	Messrs Storey & Robinson A rich silk MA gown & a Cambridge MA hood	13	12	–
6 June 1838	The Royal Mint 5 Rich Crimson Velvet Bags trimmed with silk fringe & tassels & lined with silk	11	11	–
11 June 1838	The Bishop of Worcester A rich velvet cope for the coronation			
29 May 1839	Rt. Hon. the Speaker of the House of Commons A rich damask State Robe trimmed with gold loops	147	10	–
29 March 1845	A rich Green Velvet Mantle of the Most Ancient and Most Noble Order of the Thistle for His Grace the Duke of Montrose			
15 Dec 1849	Twelve new scarlet gowns and thirteen new violet gowns for the use of the majistrates	418	0	–
19 Nov 1852	27 Mourning Cloaks of superfine black cloth for the funeral of the late Duke of Wellington	162	0	–
31 March 1859	Buckingham Palace 4 linen surplices for the choir New collars and sundrie repairs to 4 surplices	6	16	–
10 Dec 1859	Robert Laurie, Clarenceux King of Arms Tabard, velvet embroidered, lined with satin	60	0	–

The firm's name had been changed to Joseph Ede in 1848, and it continued to trade under the same name after Joseph Ede's death in 1862. His widow, Anne, now assumed control, and received a royal warrant as robemaker to Queen Victoria on 7 April 1862. Their son, Joseph Webb Ede, was then seventeen years old and already involved in the business of robemaking. There is no indication of any family relationship between the Webbs and the Edes and his middle name of Webb was probably chosen by his parents in memory of Joseph Ede's robemaking mentor.

Anne Ede did not survive her husband by many years and in 1868 Joseph Webb Ede was appointed robemaker to Queen Victoria, having taken control of the firm whose name he now changed from Joseph Ede to Ede & Son.

In 1868 a move was made from 193 Fleet Street to 93 and 94 Chancery Lane, where the firm has remained ever since. The building has a long and interesting history. The earliest lease on record concerning this property dates from 1512 when one William Malhom was granted a lease of sixty years at an annual rent of 20/- by Thomas Docwra, prior of the Hospital of St John of Jerusalem in England.

By 1541 the priory of the Hospital of St John of Jerusalem at Clerkenwell had, like so many others, been dissolved, and the Chancery Lane property passed to a new owner who leased it to the president and scholars of Magdalen College, Oxford. Shortly afterwards the college acquired the freehold and it remained their property until quite recently.

In 1824 Magdalen College commissioned a survey of 93 and 94 Chancery Lane which is described in the document as 'an Estate situate within the Liberty of the Rolls in the Parish of Saint Dunstan's in the West, London'. This survey is of interest for the details it gives of working activities in the Chancery Lane of 1824, less than fifty years before the firm moved into the street. We read that the property consisted of two brick-built dwellings, with cellar storeys, shops on the ground floor and three storeys above. To the rear were a number of small yards and several other dwellings. One of these, butting on to Star Yard, had been adapted for use as a bricklayers' shed with carpenters' shops above, while the basement, reached by means of a descending plane, was fitted out and used as a stable for six horses.

Joseph Webb Ede married in the April of 1871. His bride was Rosanna Ravenscroft, daughter of Burton Ravenscroft, who ran a successful wig-making business in nearby Serle Street. The two families would have been well known to each other. They moved in similar circles in the business world and must have had many customers in common. It was an extremely suitable match and hopes for the future would have been high. However, only six months after the marriage, in September 1871, Joseph Webb Ede died at the untimely age of twenty-six. For the third time in its history the firm was under female management and on 26 September 1871 Queen Victoria graciously confirmed the appointment of her new robemaker.

An early 19th-century engraving of 93 and 94 Chancery Lane.

A gold worker sews gold ornaments on to a robe. The ornaments are made by hand from gold wire.

At the time Rosa Ede can little have imagined that this was a position she was to hold for sixty years.

Rosa Ede was a capable, forthright woman, well able to hold her own in the world of commerce. There were times when her estimates were questioned and she was pressured to reduce her invoices, but these demands were invariably met with a polite but firm refusal. She was a great letter writer and missed no opportunity to attract new business. In her day it was quite acceptable for those in trade to approach royalty requesting the honour of a royal appointment. She wrote to members of the royal family and to European sovereigns, concluding her letters with the words, 'we may mention that we hold the Appointment as Robemakers to Her Majesty the Queen and H.R.H. the Prince of Wales'. Rosa Ede was not always successful in obtaining such appointments but she never failed to promote Ede & Son and to point out that, 'we are the oldest robemakers in London having been established in the reign of William and Mary. Our firm is of 200 years standing'.

The beginning of the 20th century saw a major change for the firm with the merger of Ede & Son with Ravenscroft, the wig maker, in 1902. Burton Ravenscroft, the oldest of Rosa Ede's four brothers, had taken over the family wig-making business in 3 Serle Street, Lincoln's Inn, and he now moved to 1 Star Yard, premises backing on to the Chancery Lane shop. Rosa Ede's brothers, Clement and Vernon, were already working with her in the robemaking business and indeed had been doing so for several decades. With the merger came a change of name. Although Rosa Ede had been widowed for over thirty years the reference to Joseph Webb Ede was retained and the firm traded as Ede, Son & Ravenscroft. It was not until 1921 that the decision was taken to change the firm's name to Ede & Ravenscroft.

The Ravenscrofts were a family of some note. They originated in Cheshire, but several branches of the family had settled in London before the end of the 17th century and in an account of the parish of St Clement Danes, written in 1876, John Diprose refers to Thomas Ravenscroft, founder of the peruke-making firm, as 'the descendant of the oldest resident family in the Parish.' The family history is well documented and contains accounts of a number of eminent and talented people.

Thomas Ravenscroft founded his wig-making business at 3 Serle Street in 1726. At the time the wearing of wigs was the height of fashion and early 18th-century paintings and, more particularly, cartoons, give some idea of the amazing and plainly ridiculous wigs that were worn. Many were said to exceed three feet in length and by contemporary standards were very expensive. Thomas Ravenscroft no doubt supplied such vanities, but while he was meeting the demands of his more extravagant customers he was also developing the market of the legal profession, and introducing the smaller, more modest wigs which were to become the established wear of members of the bench and bar.

Wigs had formed part of the formal dress of judges and barristers since about 1670. The bishops had also worn wigs on ceremonial occasions from about the same time, but they discontinued the practice during the reign of William IV. The legal wigs of the late 17th and early 18th centuries were made of black horsehair which constantly needed frizzing and curling into place. Maintaining the wigs in reasonable condition was an almost daily task, involving their being treated with pomatum, a scented ointment, and then liberally powdered. They were at best unpleasant and heavy, while the pomatum and powder shed from the curls was both unsightly and damaging to the wearer's clothes.

This state of affairs persisted throughout the 18th century, during which time the Ravenscrofts, situated as they were at the centre of legal and literary London, built up a thriving business. Thomas Ravenscroft's son, also Thomas, inherited the firm in 1750. It was this second Thomas Ravenscroft who started to collect portraits of the legal celebrities of his time. His collection was augmented by his son, Humphrey, and in even greater measure by his grandson, Burton. Over a hundred of these portraits, mainly small prints, have been preserved and form a unique record of the leading legal dignitaries of the 18th and 19th centuries.

By the early 19th century the firm was in the hands of Humphrey Ravenscroft, grandson of the founder. He was a man of considerable talent and, perhaps motivated by the monotony of frizzing, curling and powdering wigs, set about overcoming the problem. For a number of years he experimented, finally perfecting a wig made of white horsehair which he patented and offered to the public on 14 March 1822. This was his famous forensic wig, whose pattern and method of manufacture is used to the present day. It is little wonder that Humphrey Ravenscroft's wig was a success for, as the patent specification states, here was a wig

> the curls whereof are constructed on a Principal to Supersede the Necessity for Frizzing, Curling, or Using Hard Pomatum, and for forming the Curls in a Way not to be Uncurled, and also for the Tails of the Wig not to require Tying in Dressing; and, further, the Impossibility of any Person Untying them.

Following this success Humphrey Ravenscroft turned his attention to improving the full-bottomed wig, a task which occupied his talents for more than ten years. The results were published in 1835:

RAVENSCROFT,
PATENT FORENSIC WIG MAKER,
SERLE STREET, LINCOLN'S INN.

TO

The Right Honourable the Lord High Chancellor
The Right Honourable the Lord Chief Justice of the Court of King's Bench
The Right Honourable the Master of the Rolls
The Right Honourable the Vice Chancellor
The Right Honourable the Lord Chief Justice of the Court of Common Pleas
The Right Honourable the Lord Chief Baron of the Court of Exchequer
The Right Honourable the Speaker of the House of Commons
The Judges of the Ecclesiastical and Civil Courts

The Masters in Chancery	The King's Counsel
The King's Serjeants	The Serjeants at Law

The Patentee most respectfully submits his new and improved Full-Bottom Wig, which has been re-modelled and executed on an entirely new principle, the Flaps or Wings having the same uniformity of curl as the Body of the Wig, and by their peculiar construction they retain the powder and pomatum, *which will not fall out in wearing*, neither will they soil or powder the silk gowns or robes in the manner the common Full-Bottom Wigs usually do. . . .

The Patentee . . .will guarantee that the Hair of the Full-Bottom Wig shall *retain* the same uniformity of curl *all over*, so long as they can possibly be worn and dressed; and also, that the powder and pomatum will not fall *through* the Flaps or Wings; and, what is of infinite advantage, they will not in the slightest degree oppose the organ of *hearing*, . . .

The Price of the newly-invented Full-Bottom Wig, notwithstanding its superiority to the old method of construction, is no more than what is now charged for the common one – *Ten Guineas*.

BY PARTICULAR DESIRE of several eminent Law Personages, the Patentee has continued a series of experiments, for some years past, and, by unremitting assiduity, has now brought to the highest state of perfection an UNPOWDERED Full-Bottom Wig, being so near a resemblance to powder as not to be discerned by the nicest observer.

Specimens of the UNPOWDERED Full-Bottom Wig will be ready for inspection in HILARY TERM. Manufactured *only* by the Inventor and Patentee, *Price Twelve Guineas*.

January 1st, 1835.

With the introduction of his forensic wig in 1822, Humphrey Ravenscroft began to collect the signature of barristers. They were invited to sign a book when they visited 3 Serle Street to be measured for their first wig. In subsequent years the book was again produced for signature when a barrister took silk or when a QC became a judge. This practice continued over many years and the resulting twelve volumes of legal autographs,

kept among the archives, form an unusual record. The signatures run into the thousands and numerous famous names are to be found there, signing these books long before they occupied the positions which brought them to public notice. In the 19th century we find, for example, Robert Peel; H.H. Asquith, subsequently prime minister and 1st Earl of Oxford and Asquith; Charles Swinfen Eady, who became master of the rolls and later Lord Swinfen; Russell of Killowen; and Martin Archer Shee.

The list of familiar 20th-century names is so long that it is difficult to select just a few examples. We find the signatures of Patrick Hastings, Stafford Cripps, Christmas Humphreys, L. Hore-Belisha, and Quintin Hogg. J. Grimond and P. Heathcote Amory also signed the book along with Airey Neave, Ashley Bramall and Leon Brittan. In 1922 a volume was opened for the signatures of women barristers. The first signature is that of Miss Helena Normanton and many others follow including Miss D. Booth, who became a judge, Elizabeth Lane, subsequently Mrs Justice Lane, and Margaret H. Thatcher.

In addition to the volumes of legal autographs the archives contain a number of the Ravenscrofts' ledgers from the mid-19th century until about 1940, making it possible to trace the more recent activities of the firm and gain a clear picture of wig making at the time of the merger with Ede & Son.

A ledger entry on 6 March, 1903 attracts attention for being as descriptive as it is unexpected. To the account of H.I.M. the King of Portugal are entered forty-four wigs for the use of the King's coachmen in Lisbon and on his country estate. State wigs with six rows of curls were made for the first and second coachmen in Lisbon, named Baptista and Pedro, while wigs with five and three rows of curls were dispatched to ten further coachmen and fourteen postilions. The order for the country estate itemised eighteen dress wigs. Here again the individual coachmen are named and we find Pedro and Bento, the first and second coachmen, each receiving wigs with five rows of curls while wigs of four and three rows were made for the remaining six coachmen and ten postilions, among whom were Felicio, Lopez, Valentino, Santos and Andrias. Each coachman is named because, like legal wigs, each wig had to be individually fitted.

Wigs were also made for the British royal household, as well as being supplied to many private families. It is interesting to find that the number of rows of curls on a wig was used as an indication of rank: for the staff of a duke or a marquess a state wig had seven rows of curls, a house wig had six, and a carriage wig, five, while for the staff of an earl, a viscount or a baron the number of rows of curls on the state and house wigs was reduced by one. Accounts for such private individuals were numerous, among them the Compte de Castellane, Earl Spencer, Lord Rothschild, and the Duke of Wellington.

Wigs are now made almost exclusively for members of the legal profession although there remain a few civic offices which call for the wearing of a wig on ceremonial occasions.

Ede and Ravenscroft make three types of forensic wig, of which two are worn by judges. One is the full-bottomed wig, with its horizontal rows of fixed curls, which falls from the crown of the head, over the ears, and on to the shoulders. This is the wig invariably depicted in illustrations of courtroom scenes but it is, in fact, for ceremonial use only. When presiding in a court of law a judge wears a bench wig, known as the undress or tye wig. This wig is frizzed all over, with no curls, and has two small ties of horsehair at the back. The third wig is worn by barristers. Known as the bar wig, it was the subject of Humphrey Ravenscroft's invention of 1822. This wig has a frizzed crown, below which are four rows of seven curls, then one row of four curls with one curl vertically between them, and two tails, looped and tied.

The firm's wig-making department in Star Yard has seen few changes in working methods since the 19th century. Wigs continue to be made according to Humphrey Ravenscroft's patent, and the rows of shelves with the wood block models on which the wigs are constructed look just the same as they

The three types of legal wig are (from left to right) *full-bottomed, bar, and bench or tye (worn by judges).*

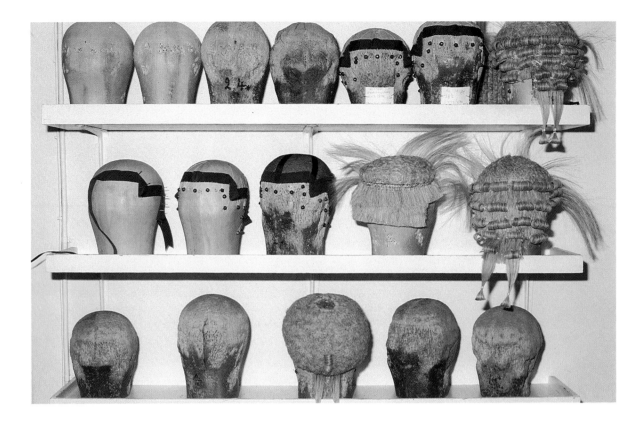

would have done in his time. Each wig is made by hand and takes four weeks to complete.

Horsehair for wig making comes from countries all over the world, including Italy, Spain, China and Japan. It is first treated against anthrax and then cleaned and bleached before being sorted into hanks and supplied to the wig makers. A small proportion of dark hairs is used in the making of each wig and this gives the slightly grey tone preferred by the lawyers who are reluctant to appear in court with a wig that looks brand new.

A feature of the wig department is the array of airtight metal cases in which judges and barristers store their wigs. These, too, have changed little over the years and are extremely smart in shiny black enamel with gold trim and the owner's name painted on them in gold letters.

More than two hundred and sixty years after Thomas Ravenscroft set up his wig-making business at Lincoln's Inn, Ede and Ravenscroft continue to supply the legal profession throughout the British Isles and overseas, particularly in Australia, Nigeria and Malaysia.

Following the merger with the Ravenscrofts the firm remained in the hands of Rosa Ede and her four brothers for twenty-five years. Burton and Ernest Ravenscroft continued to manage the wig-making department while Rosa Ede, Clement and Vernon Ravenscroft attended to the robemaking side of affairs. During these years the firm often featured in papers and magazines and an article in the *Evening News* describes the Chancery Lane shop and its activities in a way quite recognisable to those who know it today:

Parliament opens next Tuesday. Which explains why yesterday afternoon in a narrow-fronted shop that runs back from Star Yard, behind Lincoln's Inn, until it joins another shop in Chancery Lane, red cloth bags were being brought up from a camphor and cold storage basement. In these bags were the red, ermine and gold robes worn by the peers at the state opening of Parliament. The robes of half the peerage are stored in that basement. They were being brought up alphabetically. Yesterday they had reached the 'E's'. When all the robes have come up and been brushed and overhauled they will go away in carts to the House of Lords.

Behind the counter yesterday two wig makers sat at work. They had a background of shelves filled with rows of wood blocks that looked like mummified heads. They were the blocks on which barristers' and judges' wigs are made – all sizes. 'Elm is the best wood,' said Mr Ernest Ravenscroft, 'We don't get such blocks as we used to do.'

It was then I was taken to a room where are kept books which start from 1822 and contain autographs of all the famous lawyers since that date. One book was started by Lord Birkenhead when he became Lord Chancellor. Thirteen and a third pages are now occupied by the signatures of women barristers.

Lord Brampton – Mr Justice Hawkins was the last judge to wear one of the old powdered wigs. The wigs had to be powdered every day and cost a judge £8 to £10 a year. 'Lord Brampton was very careful about his wig,' said Mr Ravenscroft, 'When we sent round for it to his house in Tilney Street, he used to hand it to our man himself. He would never let his butler take charge of it.'

On the wall was a signed photograph of Lord Chief Justice Cockburn, something of a rarity. 'When I took it round to ask him to autograph it he said "I never do this" but he signed that one!'

Rosa Ede died on 4 November 1931, and on the following day all the London papers carried a short article about this remarkable woman who had held a royal warrant as robemaker for just over sixty years. During that time she had made robes for Queen Victoria, Edward VII and Queen Alexandra, George V and Queen Mary, the Prince of Wales, the Duke and Duchess of York, Princess Mary, the Duke of Gloucester and Prince George. By this time Rosa Ede's nephew, Stanley, had joined the firm, and in later years his daughter and grandson continued to run the business. The firm remained in the Ravenscroft family for some forty years before coming under new management during the 1970s.

The Royal Robes

Coronations are not frequent events but when they do occur they require an enormous amount of work by robemakers and others associated with state ceremonial. Ede and Ravenscroft have been closely involved in all the coronations which have taken place during their three-hundred-year history, and detailed notes of their work have survived in some instances.

Painstaking records were kept of the robes made for the coronation of George III in 1761. The firm made new robes for the King and the royal dukes, and the day book also shows accounts for no less than sixteen other dukes and forty-six earls. Including the other degrees of the peerage, the total is well over a hundred. A considerable number of peers invested in swords and coronets. In those days an earl's silver-gilt coronet could be purchased for thirteen guineas (but a viscount's cost fourteen guineas) and a ceremonial sword and belt cost four guineas.

opposite: George III's coronation robes, with gold brocade underdress, are particularly sumptuous. The robe itself is believed to be the oldest still in existence and is kept in the Court Dress Collection at Kensington Palace.

This striking description of George III's coronation robes is taken from the firm's day book.

35

There is a long-standing tradition among noble families of handing robes down through the generations. Some entries show that only minor repairs or alterations were necessary but other robes needed rather more drastic attention. The entry for the Countess of Peterborough's robe is brief and to the point:

1761   The Right Honourable the Countess of Peterborough
Sept 21

	£	s	d
To 3½ yards of White Sarsnet at 4s	–	14	–
To addition of Ermin and Ribbonds	–	15	–
To Pulling the Mantle to Pieces and new Making it and altering the Trimmings	1	1	–
	£ 2	10	–
1761 Sept 21 Pays in full	£ 2	10	–

An engraving from the record of George IV's coronation shows the King attended by eight eldest sons of peers, assisted by the Master of the Robes. The artist may have used some artistic licence in his depiction of the King's robes.

Sixty years later, the outstanding event in William Webb's career must surely have been the coronation of George IV, in 1821. Preparations began months in advance and, since this was to be the most lavish of all coronations, no expense was spared. William Webb had held the appointment of robemaker to George III for more than twenty years, and received a new warrant from George IV early in his reign, on 5 April 1820.

Twenty-seven tailors worked to fulfil the official orders for the coronation and it is interesting to find that William Webb is the only one to be styled 'robemaker'. He ranked third in the

list of payments, receiving a total of £2044 4s 0d, a very considerable sum in those days. The accounts are quite detailed and make fascinating reading. The majority of the work seems to have been for knights and officers of the orders of chivalry and for the officers of arms. Mantles were made for the Gentleman Usher of the Black Rod and the Gentleman Usher of the Green Rod, who are officers of the Orders of the Garter and the Thistle. Then there were mantles for forty-eight Knights Grand Cross of the Order of the Bath. William Webb bought 438½ yards of crimson satin and 367 yards of white silk mantua for the mantles while a further 288 yards of crimson satin and 276 yards of white silk mantua were required for the surcoats. Next came the Knights Commander of the Bath, one hundred in all, each requiring a mantle of the same crimson satin. There followed mantles for the kings of arms, heralds and pursuivants, including Scotland's Lord Lyon King of Arms, and for the nine officers of the College of Arms attending at the coronation. Their mantles and surcoats were of white satin with a lining of red sarsnet.

Like his predecessors, William Webb was not one to neglect the practicalities of life, as a footnote to his account attests:

1821
July 19th   Attendance of 20 Men at the Coronation to Robe
              and un-robe the Peers. Expences for Provisions and
              Boats to and from Westminster.   £43 10 6

Ede & Ravenscroft are fortunate in having in their possession a large illustrated volume giving a full account of the coronation. It was produced in 1826 and contains a large number of coloured prints taken from paintings especially commissioned at the time. The artist recorded the King and the royal dukes, the officers of state and many of the peers. Among them are two representatives of the Most Honourable Order of the Bath wearing the robes made for them by William Webb.

The coronation lived up to all expectations. Each part of that long day, the procession, the service, and later, the coronation banquet in Westminster Hall, was state ceremonial on the grand scale and must have been a breathtaking sight.

The coronations of William IV, and then of Queen Victoria, both followed relatively quickly after this great event, and would have involved much less work for the robemakers. However, when Queen Victoria died in 1901 she had been on the throne for more than sixty years. Consequently, the coronation of Edward VII was a new experience for the many people with responsibility for the arrangements.

Rosa Ede lost no time in writing to Buckingham Palace, 'soliciting the honour of making the Coronation Robes for His Majesty the King'. Permission was granted and the work was

A Knight Grand Cross of the Most Honourable Military Order of the Bath at the coronation of George IV in 1821.

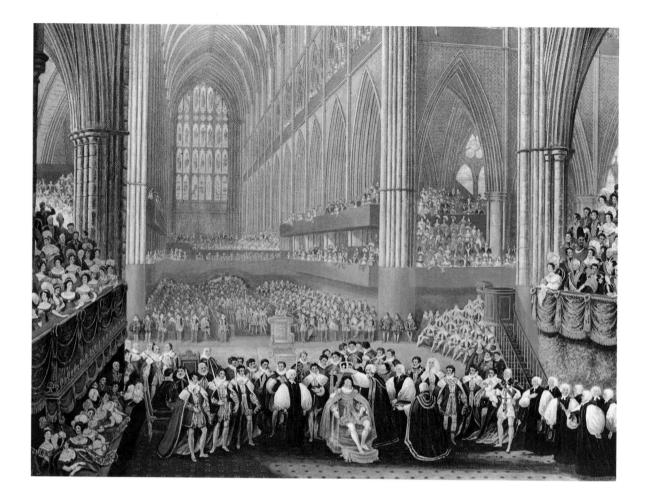

George IV's coronation service in Westminster Abbey. This was probably the last occasion on which full dress regalia, including underdress, was worn by all the participants.

immediately set in hand. The firm also sent a letter to each of the peers:

My Lord,

Coronation of His Majesty King Edward VII

We venture to write asking if we may have the honour to put your Robe and Coronet in Hand.

We make this early application in view of the great demand likely to occur and the trouble in obtaining materials as the time approaches. We gather this from what our books reveal at previous coronations for the past 200 years and the pressure at the recent opening of Parliament.

We make the Robes and Coronets as worn by the Peeresses.

Trusting to be favoured with your commands, which shall have our personal attention.

We are,

My Lord,

Your Most Obedient Servants

Ede and Son.

opposite: Edward VII, wearing military uniform under his coronation robe.

Rosa Ede's dealings with Queen Alexandra's staff appear to have been less formal. The following brief note, written by a lady-in-waiting, was sent to Ede & Son from Sandringham in February 1901:

Your letter was put before the Queen about the Coronation Robes and I think that will be alright when the time comes for them to be arranged.

The illustrated record of the coronation of Edward VII and Queen Alexandra portrays an occasion of great dignity and splendour. The officers of state, the peers, knights of the Garter, and officers of arms, were there in all the colourful grandeur of ceremonial dress. The royal coronation robes were made of magnificent purple silk velvet, the long trains heavily embroidered in gold and fully lined with best ermine.

The firm's ledger entry for work done in connection with this coronation is lengthy and gives details of the rich silk velvet used for the King's crimson and purple robes, the best white

Queen Alexandra gave Rosa Ede this picture of herself as a personal token of her appreciation. The train of the Queen's robe is richly hand-embroidered with gold bullion.

The coronation robes of George V and Queen Mary were adapted from those recently made for the coronation of Edward VII and Queen Alexandra.

cambric for the Colobium Sindonis, and crimson silk lining for the cloth-of-gold dalmatic and imperial mantles. It appears that Ede & Son were responsible for most of the robemaking and the account includes robes for many officers of state, as well as for bishops and clergy. It goes on to list such items as the gold-fringed scarlet altar cloths and yards of crimson velvet to upholster the coronation chairs.

After the coronation Rosa Ede received a splendid framed print of Queen Alexandra in her coronation robes. Signed by the Queen herself, it is known to have been Rosa Ede's most treasured possession. This picture, its gilt frame surmounted by a small crown, remains on display at Ede & Ravenscroft to the present day.

King Edward VII died in 1910 and the country prepared for a second coronation in less than ten years. The coronation robes made by the firm for Edward VII and Queen Alexandra were on exhibition at the Tower of London. Since they were practically new it was decided to make the necessary adjustments and use them for the coronation of George V and Queen Mary. This presented no problem to Ede, Son & Ravenscroft who reported on 6 January 1911 that

The alterations which Their Majesties may require can easily be prepared beforehand as we still possess our patterns from which the Two Robes and cloth of gold were cut and made. Time will chiefly be required for the gold lace embroidery to be renovated by our special process as we are now doing for one of His Majesty's Robes.

There was little robemaking to be done prior to this coronation, understandably so considering the short time that had elapsed since Edward VII had been crowned. Comparing pictures of the two events it is clear that many of the same individuals played their part as officers of state on both occasions.

After the coronation of George V and Queen Mary on 22 June 1911 the coronation robes were included among the exhibits at the newly established London Museum where strict procedures were observed for the security of such valuable items. However, by 1915 the coronation robes were back in the firm's workroom undergoing treatment for the ravages of the clothes moth. The Assistant Secretary of the London Museum, alarmed by events, wrote to Mrs Ede telling her that the Keeper of the Museum

would be glad to know your opinion as to how this moth originated, if possible, and to what extent its ravages have taken.

Rosa Ede replied immediately and at some length:

In reply to your esteemed favour with reference to the Coronation Robes which we are freeing from moth and hope to return within three weeks. We cannot tell what damage has been done to the fur until taken off and baked.

It is impossible to say how the moth originated, it may be on account of the case not being airtight as they will get into the very smallest crevices and when the eggs are once deposited speedily produce the grub which starts the mischief and then becomes another moth, as this process goes on indefinitely during hot weather the damage is very soon apparent.

We would suggest as a preventative in the future the liberal use of Napthaline, the manufacturers of this tell us that as far as their knowledge goes they do not think it would harm the Embroidery.

A second precaution is to carefully paint all the crevices and beadings with a poorish class of paint mostly Terpentine on account of its pungent odour.

To make sure that the case is thoroughly cleared of eggs it would be well to fumigate with sulphur.

The Robes should be carefully combed occasionally.

Any further particulars we shall be pleased to furnish you with.

At the time of George V's coronation Ede, Son & Ravenscroft were robemakers to the young Prince of Wales, making the

The Prince of Wales, later Edward VIII, with his sister, the Princess Royal, dressed for the coronation of their parents in 1911. The Prince of Wales is wearing the robes of a Knight of the Garter.

George VI and Queen Elizabeth, with their children, Princess Elizabeth and Princess Margaret, after the coronation in 1937.

Garter robe which he wore at the coronation, as well as the purple velvet robe for his investiture at Caernarvon in 1911. After the death of George V in January 1936 they received the appointment of robemaker to His Majesty King Edward VIII. Edward VIII was king for eleven months only, and was never crowned, abdicating on 10 December 1936. He was succeeded by his younger brother the Duke of York. The date already chosen for the coronation was allowed to stand and King George VI and Queen Elizabeth were crowned on 12 May 1937.

As in previous years the firm did a great deal of robemaking for the coronation and the ledgers give an account of the robes made for the King and Queen and also the small robes especially designed for the young Princess Elizabeth and her sister, Princess Margaret Rose.

Her Royal Highness Princess Elizabeth succeeded to the throne on the death of her father on 6 February 1952. Within a few months the royal robemakers were making plans for the coronation. Each coronation has been marked by the great attention paid to every detail of correct dress. As arrangements were under way for the coronation of Queen Elizabeth II the firm's advice was sought on many aspects of dress by those preparing to attend the ceremony, and the firm entered into

correspondence with the Earl Marshal's office regarding the correct wear for peers and knights of the orders of chivalry at the coronation. Bluemantle Pursuivant of Arms replied:

> Those peers in the Procession inside the Abbey who are Knights of the Garter, The Thistle or St. Patrick, may wear mantles of those Orders instead of Robes of State, but they may not wear the mantles of any other Orders of Chivalry unless they are representing those Orders in the Procession. They may not wear Parliamentary Robes in the Procession. If they are not in the Procession they may wear the mantle of any Order of Knighthood so long as it is their senior Order.

Bluemantle also sent the firm a complete set of 'Dress Regulations for a Coronation', a series of leaflets issued by the Earl Marshal giving details of all the different forms of ceremonial dress seen in Westminster Abbey on this great state occasion.

The ledger entry for the coronation robes for Her Majesty Queen Elizabeth II echoes those of previous coronations through the centuries:

1952
July 23

> Making and supplying Imperial State Robe for the Coronation of Her Majesty Queen Elizabeth II being a six yard train in best quality hand made purple silk velvet, trimmed with best quality Canadian ermine 5" on top and underside and fully lined with pure silk English Satin complete with Ermine cape and all being tailed ermine in the traditional manner and including embroidery by the Royal School of Needlework.
> Making and supplying Parliamentary Robe for Her Majesty Queen Elizabeth II in the best quality hand made crimson velvet trimmed with gold lace in the traditional manner and lined throughout with finest Canadian ermine.

His Royal Highness the Duke of Edinburgh also had robes made for the coronation:

1952
August 21

> A Royal Dukes Coronation Robe in the best hand made silk velvet trimmed with finest Canadian ermine. Coronet in metal gilt with airtight case with name inscribed. A pages uniform complete.

Pages attending the peers wear a variety of colours, each adopting the livery colour of the peer they accompany. Scarlet is the exception, as the regulation states:

At her coronation in 1953, H.M. Queen Elizabeth II wore a purple velvet robe, trimmed with ermine and embroidered in gold with olives and acorns, symbols of peace and prosperity. Her white satin dress was embroidered with the symbols of England, Wales, Ireland, Scotland, and the countries of the Commonwealth.

The coats should be of the first livery colour except where the livery colour is scarlet when a variant such as claret colour or murrey should be used. When the second livery colour is white the lace, buttons and buckles should be silver.

Pages' outfits are very colourful and attractive, with white knee breeches and silk stockings, shoes of black patent leather with scarlet heels and gilt or silver buckles, and gilt or silver buttons, 'struck with the Peer's Crest, Arms, Badge or Cypher'. Each page also has 'a short sword with cross guard and horse's head pommel, ivory grip, and white leather scabbard with gilt mount'.

A coronation is without doubt the greatest of our state ceremonies and one which demonstrates in a unique way the long history and continuity of the British monarchy. It is at once a solemn and an exultant occasion. The coronation of Her Majesty Queen Elizabeth II was made all the more moving by the fact that, through the medium of television, it was shared by the whole nation.

In 1958 His Royal Highness the Prince Charles was created Prince of Wales. At the time the Queen made a pledge to the Welsh people that she would present him to them at Caernarvon when he had grown up. Nine years later on 18 May 1967 it was announced that the investiture of the Prince of Wales was to take place at Caernarvon Castle on 1 July 1969.

Ede & Ravenscroft set in hand the making of a new robe for the Prince of Wales. This was to be of similar style to the one worn by his predecessor in 1911. A ledger entry of 6 August 1967 describes the Prince of Wales' ceremonial dress for the investiture:

> The robe of hand woven purple velvet trimmed with fleur de lys embroidery all round including the train, ermine cape and collar fully lined with white silk and the inside facings of the robe lined with ermine to an extent of 10" in width.

The fleur de lys embroidery on the new robe was to a new design which resembled more closely the Prince of Wales' feathers but, in keeping with tradition, the solid gold clasps fastening the robe were the ones used in 1911 by the previous Prince of Wales.

Robes for Peers and Parliament

The structured order of the varying degrees of peers' ranks and titles as we know them today, each with its appropriate distinguishing marks, developed slowly over the course of several centuries. Certainly during the 14th century ceremonies of the investiture of peers took place in the presence of the sovereign and in subsequent years we read of dukes, marquesses and earls being invested with swords, caps of estate, coronets and robes of estate. This robe of estate, given to a peer at his investiture and thereafter worn only at a coronation, was the forerunner of the present coronation robe which resembles it closely in design and materials. It was a full-length robe of crimson velvet, cut slightly longer at the back to give the effect of a small train. It was edged with miniver fur and had a small cape, also of miniver, which carried the rows of ermine tails denoting a peer's rank. The use of rows of sealskin spots to differentiate the robes according to rank continues to this day. The rows extend around the full width of the cape, with the half rows extending from the right front edge to the centre back. The number of rows for the different degrees is:

4   for a Duke
3½ for a Marquess
3   for an Earl
2½ for a Viscount
2   for a Baron

Peeresses' coronation robes are of the same crimson velvet but are very different in style. Instead of the peers' edge-to-edge robe with its miniver cape, the peeresses' robe is close fitting, open down the front, and has short fitted sleeves, a small cape across the shoulders, and a train. The front edge of the robe and the sleeves are edged with miniver fur while the train has an edging of ermine. Peeresses' robes also vary according to rank and in their case, in addition to the rows of sealskin spots on the cape, it is the length of the train and the width of the ermine edging which denotes their degree of peerage. For a duchess the train is 2 yards in length and has a 5-inch ermine

opposite: The Earl of Lichfield wearing his coronation robe and holding the coronet. His rank is indicated by the three rows of sealskin spots on the ermine cape and by the design of the coronet. The robe is made of crimson velvet, fully lined with white satin.

The Duchess of Buccleuch, Mistress of the Robes at the coronation of Edward VII, with her page.

edging; for a marchioness, a 1¾-yard train and a 4-inch ermine edging; for a countess, a 1½-yard train with a 3-inch edging; for a viscountess, a 1¼-yard train with a 2-inch edging; and for a baroness, a 1-yard train with a 2-inch edging.

The ranks of peers and peeresses are also shown by the style of their coronets of degree, which vary considerably in their design. Each coronet has a crimson velvet lining with a gold tassel and a band of ermine around the base. This is in fact the old cap of estate but for the best part of three hundred years the two have been combined. The peers' coronets are:

Coronet of a Duke	A gold circlet with 8 strawberry leaves
Coronet of a Marquess	A silver-gilt circlet with 4 strawberry leaves alternating with 4 silver balls a little raised on points
Coronet of an Earl	A silver-gilt circlet with 8 strawberry leaves alternating with 8 silver balls raised on points
Coronet of a Viscount	A silver-gilt circlet with 16 silver balls set on the rim
Coronet of a Baron	A silver-gilt circlet with 6 silver balls set on the rim

Peeresses' coronets are identical in design to those of the peers but are considerably smaller, being made to sit on the top of the head.

A drawing of the peers' coronets from the Earl Marshal's regulations for the coronation of H.M. Queen Elizabeth II. They are (from left to right, top row) those of a duke, marquess and earl, and (bottom row) viscount and baron.

Coronets of degree are worn only at a coronation and there are clear procedures to be followed. The peers carry their coronets until that central moment when St Edward's Crown is placed on the sovereign's head and then they each put on their coronets, wearing them for the remainder of the service. At the coronation of Elizabeth II in 1953 the peeresses put on their coronets at the same moment as the peers but when a king is crowned the peeresses must wait for the moment of crowning

of the queen consort. This was the case at the coronation of George VI and Queen Elizabeth in 1937.

The peers' parliamentary robe was introduced during the 15th century and has changed very little since then. It is a full-length robe of finely woven scarlet wool with a collar and edging of white miniver fur, and is worn over a morning suit. The side seams of the robe are open and the different degrees of the peerage are indicated by the number of miniver bars, which extend from the right front edge of the robe to the side seam and from the side seam round to the centre back. Each bar of miniver is three inches wide and is edged with a two-inch band of gold lace. The number of miniver bars for the various degrees follows the same order as for the peers' coronation robes:

A group of peers wearing their parliamentary robes, on which their rank is indicated by the number of ermine bars. They are (from left to right) The Viscount Torrington, The Earl of Shrewsbury and Waterford, The Duke of Norfolk, The Marquess of Reading and The Baron Stafford.

<pre>
4   for a Duke
3½ for a Marquess
3   for an Earl
2½ for a Viscount
2   for a Baron
</pre>

Parliamentary robes have formed a part of Ede and Ravenscroft's business throughout the firm's history and the following account is taken from the Shudalls' day book:

<pre>
1760   His Grace the Duke of Marlborough
Feb 25
                                                £   s   d
          To 7 yards of Superfine Scarlet Wool
          Cloth at 21s   7   7   –
          To 20 yards of White Sarsnet at 4s   4   –   –
          To the Choicest of Ermins   16 16   –
          To 16oz of Gold Orriss at 10s   8   –   –
          To Making the Robe   5   –   –
          To 1 yard of Superfine Scarlet Cloth for
          the Bag   1   1   –
          To 4 yards of White Sarsnet at 4s   16   –
          To a set of Rich Silk Tassels and Cord 1   1   –
          To Making the Bag   5   –
                                               _____
                                              £44   6   –

          1760
          Apr 24   Pays in full   £44   6   –
</pre>

Many of the parliamentary robes worn by hereditary peers were made over a century ago. They are carefully maintained, refurbished and altered as required, and replaced only rarely. It is a matter of pride to wear a robe that is obviously of some antiquity, and the firm's records give many examples of alterations being made over the years. The following entry to the Earl of Abercorn's account also dates from Mrs Shudall's time:

<pre>
1761   The Right Honourable the Earl of Abercorn
Oct 24
                                                £   s   d
          To altering your Lordships Barons
          Parliament Robe to an Earls and White
          Ribbonds   15   –
          To one bar of Ermin   1 12   –
          To 1½ yards of gold lace at 20s for
          one Bar   1 10   –
                                               _____
                                               £3 17   –

          1761
          Oct 24   Pays in full   £3 17   –
</pre>

The State Opening of Parliament

Peers and peeresses usually wear their ceremonial dress only when the sovereign is present and consequently there are only two occasions when they assemble *en masse* wearing their robes. One is a coronation, and the other is the state opening of Parliament, when the peers gather in the House of Lords to hear the Queen's speech from the throne. The state opening normally takes place either in November, at the start of the new parliamentary session, or immediately after a General Election.

Each peer attending the state opening must wear a parliamentary robe and some four hundred peers leave their robes in the safekeeping of Ede and Ravenscroft. Behind the scenes at Chancery Lane this is a busy time of year. About a month before the ceremony letters are sent out to each of the peers whose robes are in store asking if they plan to attend and in the intervening weeks the robes are checked and carefully labelled and packed for delivery to the House of Lords. The heralds' tabards, together with their wands of office and collars (as chains of office are known), and the collars for various members of the orders of chivalry, are also collected from the Central Chancery of the Orders of Knighthood for delivery to the Peers' Library.

On the day itself a dozen or more members of staff are required to assist the peers and officers of state to robe for this great state occasion. Some of the staff make their way to the Library to await the arrival of the peers whose robes are waiting in alphabetical order on the hanging rails. Two of the firm's tailors dress the royal pages who will later carry the Queen's train, while in the Salisbury Room the heralds are assisted with their tabards and insignia. Senior members of Ede and Ravenscroft are on duty in the robing room, where the royal dukes are robed, and also in the Norman porch where the Earl Marshal and other officers of state are robed as they arrive at the House.

The state opening of Parliament is one of the great state ceremonies, a glittering occasion, displaying to the full the splendour of ceremonial dress. Her Majesty the Queen rides in state from Buckingham Palace to arrive at the royal entrance to the Palace of Westminster. There the royal staircase leads to the Norman porch and the robing room. The procession which later makes its way from the robing room through the Royal Gallery, the Prince's Chamber, and into the House of Lords is one of real magnificence. Her Majesty the Queen wears the crimson and gold parliamentary robe and the Imperial State Crown with its three thousand and more diamonds. Around her are the great officers of state resplendent in full ceremonial dress: the Earl Marshal of England in his parliamentary robes and insignia of the Most Noble Order of the Garter, and the

H.M. the Queen receives a copy of her speech from the Lord Chancellor at the State Opening of Parliament.

opposite: *The Speaker of the House of Commons, the Rt Hon. Bernard Weatherill, in full dress regalia.*

Lord Great Chamberlain in splendid scarlet and gold uniform. The Lord Chancellor, in black and gold robe and full-bottomed wig, carries the purse containing the Great Seal of England.

In the House of Lords await the Lords Temporal and the Lords Spiritual: the hereditary and life peers, and the bishops. The judges, too, are there, grouped together in scarlet robes and full-bottomed wigs. The peeresses wait in long evening dresses and tiaras. Invited guests, among them the ambassadors and diplomats of foreign countries, are also in attendance.

Her Majesty's procession reaches the chamber of the House of Lords and when all have taken their places, Black Rod, at the Queen's request, summons the House of Commons to the Bar of the House of Lords. Her Majesty the Queen then reads the Gracious Speech from the Throne, which sets out the programme of legislation to be introduced during the forthcoming session of Parliament.

No one witnessing such a magnificent scene could doubt the very great contribution made to it by the ceremonial dress. The quality and richness of the materials employed are outstanding. Velvet, silk, satin, and taffeta, almost always of silk, form the basis of much robemaking, with decoration of gold lace and embroidery, cords, tassels and ornaments. Fur is also used: ermine, miniver, sable, musquash and bear. The colours are bold and regal, ranging through scarlet, crimson, cerise, purple, pink, royal blue, dark blues and greens, to white, gold and black.

The peers assembled in the House of Lords in their parliamentary robes for the State Opening of Parliament.

The Ceremony of Introduction

Apart from the state opening of Parliament, there are three other occasions when a small number of peers, representing a royal commission, may appear in their parliamentary robes to enact a brief ceremony. These are the introduction of a new peer to the House of Lords, the election of the Speaker of the House of Commons, and the prorogation of Parliament. The most frequent of these three ceremonies is the ceremony of introduction, when a peer takes his or her seat in the House of Lords for the first time.

The present ceremony of introduction dates from 1621 and replaced the earlier ceremony of investiture which lapsed after the reign of James I. This short ceremony, lasting no more than fifteen minutes, takes place in the House of Lords in the presence of the Lord Chancellor who is seated on the Woolsack and wears his black and gold gown and a full-bottomed wig surmounted by a black tricorn hat. The new peer, carrying his writ of summons, enters the chamber with his sponsors, two peers of his own rank, all three wearing parliamentary robes and carrying black cocked hats. They are preceded by Black

H.R.H. Prince Andrew, accompanied by his two sponsors, the Duke of Gloucester (left) and the Duke of Kent, after his introduction to the House of Lords as Duke of York on 11 February 1987. The cocked hats are only worn at this ceremony.

56

The Gentleman Usher of the Black Rod, Air Chief Marshal Sir John Gingell, wearing a court coat, vest and breeches, with full lace jabot and cuffs.

Rod and by Garter King of Arms, who carries the new peer's patent of creation of peerage. Occasionally the Earl Marshal and the Lord Great Chamberlain also participate. This small procession makes its way through the chamber, bowing at three separate points to the Cloth of Estate and taking up position around the Woolsack. The new peer presents his writ of summons and his patent, which he receives from Garter, to the Lord Chancellor who hands them to the Reading Clerk; the latter takes them to the table and reads them aloud. The new peer makes his Oath of Allegiance and signs the Roll. He is then conducted by Garter to his appropriate place on the benches of the House, takes his seat between his two sponsors, and all three don their cocked hats. They then rise and doff their hats to the Chancellor who raises his tricorn hat in acknowledgement. This salutation is made three times in all and marks the end of the brief ceremony.

The Earl Marshal and the College of Arms

The Earl Marshal of England has overall responsibility for state ceremonial. In marshalling all state processions he is ably assisted and advised by the heralds. These officers of the College of Arms – kings of arms, heralds and pursuivants – are a familiar sight on many state occasions. Their distinctive tabards, medieval in style and vividly coloured in scarlet, gold and blue, show the quartered royal arms and give an indication of the long standing and importance of their office.

In ancient days it was customary for feudal nobles to employ a herald to organise the ceremonial reception of important

opposite: The Earl Marshal, the Duke of Norfolk, in full ceremonial dress of scarlet and gold coatee, doeskin breeches, white stockings and buckled shoes.

The officers of the College of Arms precede the Knights of the Garter in the annual Garter procession.

The College of Arms with H.M. the Queen and H.R.H. the Duke of Edinburgh. The officers of the College of Arms are wearing their full ceremonial dress of scarlet coatees, black breeches, black stockings and gilt-buckled shoes. Their rank is indicated by the amount of gold embroidery on their coatees.

visitors and the entertainment of guests. Later, when military tournaments were introduced, it was the herald who was sent out to proclaim the event and then, wearing his feudal lord's coat of arms, to marshal proceedings on the field. In those days there were many heralds, each acting independently on behalf of his feudal master and wearing, on ceremonial occasions, his master's coat of arms. There were also royal heralds. The principal of these became known as kings of heralds during the reign of Edward I and later as kings of arms. By the late 15th century the kings of arms and the heralds of the royal dukes and leading nobility had achieved the status of diplomats, the kings of arms acting as emissaries of the king and undertaking diplomatic missions abroad. By this time they were also expert in the etiquette of chivalry and in the keeping of registers recording the armorial bearings of the nobility and giving details of their genealogies.

The tabard came into general use in the 15th century, when it would have been made of wool and probably lined with fur. With its almost rectangular front and back panels, and straight, wide sleeve pieces, or wings, the tabard is ideal for displaying arms and was retained by the heralds when it went out of popular fashion. By the mid-15th century rules had been laid down governing the materials to be used, which were satin for the kings of arms, damask for the heralds, and sarsnet, a type of silk, for pursuivants. These materials provided the background for the royal arms which, at that time, showed the arms of England quartered with those of France. During the reign of Elizabeth I, kings of arms were ordered to wear velvet instead of satin, and fairly soon afterwards, in the reign of James I, the background for the heralds' tabards was changed from damask to satin. This established the specification which has been in use for over three hundred and fifty years, though the tabards are now quartered with the royal arms of Britain.

There have been few major changes in the heralds' ceremonial dress since the accession of William IV in 1830, when court dress swung away from the flamboyant grandeur of George IV's reign. A royal warrant of William IV in 1831 authorised a dark blue military-style uniform which was worn by the heralds for some twenty years. In 1849 Queen Victoria introduced the scarlet coatee with its blue-black velvet stand collar, cuffs and pocket flaps, and its lavish gold embroidery, which remains the full dress uniform of the heralds. The blue trousers with the gold oakleaf lace stripe on the side seams, worn with plain black patent leather boots, which were worn throughout Queen Victoria's reign, are still part of the levee dress but no longer form part of the full dress uniform. They were replaced under a royal warrant of Edward VII who ordered that black breeches, black silk stockings and black gilt-buckled shoes should be worn with the scarlet coatee on ceremonial occasions. This is still the ceremonial dress of the officers of the College of Arms. The exceptional use of white breeches and stockings with black gilt-buckled shoes is confined to coronations and this dress also dates from the time of Edward VII.

Many of the heralds' ceremonial tabards in use today were made more than a century ago and are a tribute to the craftsmanship of their creators. The royal arms are displayed four times on each tabard: on the front and back, and on both the sleeve wings. Much of the intricate sewing and the gold working of the emblems is done by hand and the fabrics are of the finest quality, with the silk for velvets, satins and damasks especially dyed to achieve the correct shade.

Ede & Ravenscroft's record of service to the officers of the College of Arms goes back some two hundred years and the archives contain numerous references to work done for successive kings of arms, heralds and pursuivants. For example, there is an original estimate of 1823, handwritten by William Webb, for a coat of arms for Robert Laurie who was at that time Rouge Croix Pursuivant. This estimate, not to exceed fifty-five pounds, was accepted by Robert Laurie and bears his initials.

Another interesting document dating from the mid-1880s is a pen and ink pattern for a tabard showing the royal arms as approved by the College of Arms in 1883. The drawing was accompanied by a detailed specification setting out the materials and decoration for pursuivants' tabards:

The Deputy Garter King of Arms (an office which is now obsolete), William Weldon, at the coronation of Edward VII. Behind, four Knights of the Garter hold the canopy for the King's anointing.

Pursuivant's Coat

A Coat of Arms of Damask Silk
lined with Crimson Sarsnet,
richly embroidered to Design.

The Quarterings of England
of Crimson Silk Damask embroidered
on Yellow Satin partially enriched
with Gold Bullion Wire edged
and ornamented with Yellow Cord
and Gold Twist.

The Quartering of Scotland, Yellow
Satin embroidered on Crimson Satin
partially enriched with Gold Bullion
Wire, edged with Yellow Silk Cord and
Gold Twist. The Quartering bordered
with Crimson Silk Cord and
Floss Silk ornaments edged with
Yellow Silk Cord and Gold
Twist.

The Quartering of Ireland on
Blue Watered Damask Silk,
embroidered on Yellow Satin partially
enriched with Gold Bullion Wire,
edged and ornamented with
Yellow Cord and Gold Twist,
the Strings of the Harp of White
Silk Cord with Silver Twist.

The Quarterings edged with a
Double Row of Gold Gimp and
black Silk Cord. The whole of
the Embroidered Devices edged
with black Silk Cord.

*A late 19th-century drawing
of a pursuivant's tabard.*

When the heralds' tabards are not in use they are stored at St James's Palace in the safekeeping of the Central Chancery of the Orders of Knighthood. There they are inspected regularly to ensure that all necessary repairs are carried out and the tabards kept in readiness for the many state occasions attended by the heralds. These include such events as the state opening of Parliament and the annual Garter ceremony at Windsor. Great care is taken to maintain each individual tabard, but from time to time it becomes necessary to take stock. During the 1970s Ede & Ravenscroft were asked to give their professional opinion on the condition of fourteen tabards. The correspondence between the firm and the Central Chancery of the Orders of Knighthood is fascinating and provides a 'behind the scenes' glimpse of the work involved.

Portcullis Pursuivant of Arms' tabard has the royal arms quartered on grounds of blue and scarlet flowered damask and yellow satin.

Of the fourteen tabards in question those of Clarenceux King of Arms, Windsor Herald and Portcullis Pursuivant were found to be in good repair and not in need of any renovation. Ede & Ravenscroft reported to Central Chancery on the remaining eleven.

Norroy and Ulster King of Arms

This tabard is in fair condition and can be used for another year, after that it will need new Velvet, Ribbons, Bows and Protective Lining; this work will be done by using the existing Emblems .... £165. 9. 6.

Chester Herald

This is in good condition, except for one Blue Satin quarter on one Wing – To re-newing Satin and replacing Emblems .... £ 26. 5. 0.

Lancaster Herald

This one needs part stripping down and most of the Blue and Red Satin replaced, new lining and Bows and Ribbons are required .... £129.13. 0.

Somerset Herald

To part stripping down and supplying new
cloth of Gold, re-lining, new Bows and
re-sewing in certain places .... £ 89.11. 6.

York Herald

In reasonably good condition, apart from
new Ribbons and Bows, and generally 'looking
over' .... £ 8.11. 6.

Arundel Herald Extrordinary

Completely overhauling and re-newing all
Velvet and Cloth of Gold and lining,
new Bows and Ribbons are required, but
part of the old braid can be re-used .... £228.10. 0.

Norfolk Herald Extraordinary

This requires part stripping down and
supplying new Red and Blue Satin Wings, new
Bows and Ribbons, and generally 'looking
over' .... £ 95.13. 9.

Bluemantle Pursuivant

Replacing the Blue Damask quarters and
generally 'looking over' .... £ 71. 0. 8.

Rouge Dragon Pursuivant

In fair condition, but needs new Bows and
Protective lining, and a certain amount of
re-sewing is necesary .... £ 17.10. 0.

Rouge Croix Pursuivant

To generally 'looking over', pressing Bows
and supplying Protective lining .... £ 21. 7. 6.

Fitzalan Pursuivant Extraordinary

In good condition, but needs a certain amount
of sewing and generally 'looking over', also
a Protective lining is required .... £ 21. 2. 9.

Occasionally a tabard reaches the stage when further renovation is impossible and this was the case in 1970 when Ede & Ravenscroft were asked by the Central Chancery to submit an estimate for repairs to the tabard of Garter Principal King of Arms.

Our examination has shown that there is little more we can do to this Tabard without completely remaking, supplying new Braids, Velvets and Cloth of Gold, but re-using the Emblems, and the work we envisage would put the Tabard into an almost new condition.

The cost of the above would be .... £240.10. 6.

Lord Lyon King of Arms, his velvet tabard quartered with the arms of Scotland.

This estimate was accepted by Her Majesty's Treasury and the resulting new tabard, with the re-use of existing emblems which in all probability date back to the early 19th century, is the one worn on ceremonial occasions by the present Garter King of Arms.

It is rare for a completely new tabard to be made. The most recent was commissioned in 1972 for Maltravers Herald of Arms. It is an outstanding example of the craftsmen's skills, and one of which Ede & Ravenscroft are justly proud.

Norroy and Ulster King of Arms, wearing his tabard of blue and crimson velvet and cloth of gold.

The Orders of Chivalry

The history of particular ancient orders of chivalry is often obscure, but it seems that the giving of rewards to loyal and devoted subjects has been the practice of monarchs from time immemorial. During the Middle Ages, gifts of land or money were gradually replaced or supplemented by awards of knighthoods with their associated insignia, including chains of honour, known as collars. The present orders of chivalry have evolved from this medieval honours system.

The Most Noble Order of the Garter was founded by Edward III in the latter half of the 14th century. It is the greatest accolade bestowed by the sovereign, an honour held in the highest regard.

During Queen Victoria's reign many European sovereigns were admitted to the Most Noble Order of the Garter and the firm's ledgers contain numerous accounts giving details of the items supplied to newly appointed knights. It is an interesting catalogue of mantles, swords and belts, white kid gloves, white kid shoes, rich velvet silk hats, and flowing hair curls. Trunks for the safekeeping of robes, particularly those sent abroad, were requested by knights of the Garter and many accounts include

A Strong Robe Trunk, covered with Garter Blue leather and an inscription plate, brass bound and nailed with a Chubb Patent Lock.

These accounts spanning sixty years are contained in a number of volumes and selecting the sovereigns of other countries alone provides an impressive list.

1842   His Majesty the King of Saxony
1844   His Royal Highness Ernest the Second, the Reigning Duke of Saxe Coburg and Gotha
1855   The Emperor of the French
1856   His Majesty the King of Sardinia
1858   His Royal Highness Prince Frederick William of Prussia

opposite: *The Most Noble Order of the Garter.*

1858	His Majesty the King of Portugal
1861	His Majesty the King of Prussia
1862	His Royal Highness Prince Louis of Hesse
1865	His Majesty the King of Denmark
1865	His Majesty the King of Portugal
1865	His Royal Highness the Grand Duke of Hesse
1873	The Shah of Persia
1876	His Majesty the King of the Hellenes
1878	His Majesty the King of Italy
1881	His Majesty Alexander III Emperor of Russia
1881	His Majesty the King of Sweden
1881	His Majesty the King of Spain
1882	His Majesty William III King of the Netherlands
1888	His Royal Highness the Crown Prince of Austria

The privilege of attending on the occasion of a Chapter of the Order of the Garter, to assist the knights companion and officers of the order to robe, has been enjoyed by the firm throughout its history. Nowadays, the Garter ceremony is usually an annual event held at Windsor Castle during the month of June. In Ede and Ravenscroft's calendar this is an important day commencing early in the morning when some twelve representatives of the firm arrive at the Castle. There they begin the task of setting out the robes and insignia in readiness for the arrival of Her Majesty the Queen and members of the royal family, the royal pages, knights companion, officers of the order, and the officers of arms.

When there are new knights companion to be admitted to the order an investiture ceremony is held in the Throne Room of Windsor Castle, where the knights companion and officers of the order assemble to await the arrival of the Queen. Then, on the Queen's instruction, two officers of the order, Garter King of Arms and the Gentleman Usher of the Black Rod, summon the knights-elect and conduct them to their places. Each knight-elect is called in turn and conducted to the Queen who invests him with the insignia of the order. First there is the garter. This is of deep-blue velvet and carries in solid gold letters that most famous of mottoes: *Honi soit qui mal y pense*. Literally translated this means 'Dishonoured be he who thinks evil of it', but the meaning intended by this motto and the reason for the choice of the garter as the central feature of the order's insignia are both obscure. Then there is the blue riband and the star with its red enamel cross of St George surrounded by the garter and motto. The knight-elect next receives the mantle. This is of the finest quality deep-blue silk velvet, with white satin ribbons and a lining of white taffeta. On the left side of the mantle is the badge of the order: the cross of St George encircled by the garter and motto. And lastly, the knight-elect is invested with the collar and the George, a badge representing St George which hangs from the collar.

The investiture is followed by a luncheon, after which the officers of arms marshal the Garter procession. This fine example of pageantry, splendidly colourful, invariably attracts a large crowd to watch Her Majesty the Queen walk in procession with her Knights of the Garter. They make their way from the Grand Entrance to Windsor Castle, down through the Norman Gate, the Middle and Lower Wards, and the gateway of the Horseshoe Cloister, to St George's Chapel for the install-

H.M. the Queen, Sovereign of the Most Noble Order of the Garter, at Windsor Castle.

Two newly invested Knights of the Garter (the Marquess of Normanby and Lord Carrington) lead the Garter procession in 1983. The 'hoods' on their right shoulders are a residual form of the original hoods, which were replaced by a flat velvet cap in 1556.

Officers of the Order of the Garter (from left to right), the Secretary, Black Rod, the Garter King of Arms, and the Dean of Windsor (who wears a purple robe).

ation service. There the Knights Companion newly invested are installed, enacting their part in the tradition of this most noble order which dates back over six hundred years. The spirit of the order is fittingly epitomised in one of the prayers of thanksgiving used each year in the order of service.

Almighty God, in whose sight a thousand years are but as yesterday; We give thee most humble and hearty thanks for that thou didst put it into the heart of thy servant, King Edward, to found this order of Christian chivalry, and hath preserved and prospered it through the centuries unto this day. And we pray that, rejoicing in thy goodness, we may bear our part with those illustrious Companions who have witnessed to thy truth and upheld thine honour, through the grace of our Lord Jesus Christ, himself the source and pattern of true chivalry; who with thee and the Holy Spirit liveth and reigneth, ever One God, world without end. Amen.

The Most Ancient and Most Noble Order of the Thistle became an established order of chivalry in 1687, but James II made it clear that he believed he was not founding a new order but reviving an ancient companionship of knights. Some sources claim that the Order of the Thistle originated as early as the 9th century but there does not seem to be any substantial evidence to support this theory.

Lord McFadzean wearing the mantle and collar of the Most Ancient and Most Noble Order of the Thistle. The mantle is of dark green velvet, fully lined with white silk, with a hood and sash of garter blue. The motto of the order is Nemo me impune lacessit *(No one provokes me with impunity).*

The Most Ancient and Most Noble Order of the Thistle

The Most Illustrious Order of Saint Patrick

The Most Honourable Order of the Bath

The Most Distinguished Order of Saint Michael and St George

The Most Exalted Order of the Star of India

The Most Eminent Order of the Indian Empire

The Royal Victorian Order

The Most Excellent Order of the British Empire

73

The Order of the Thistle is the highest honour awarded to Scottish peers, and the chapel of the order is at St Giles' Cathedral in Edinburgh where a service is normally held each year. The Knights of the Thistle wear a mantle of dark green velvet lined with white taffeta and fastened with tasselled cordons of green and gold.

The Most Illustrious Order of Saint Patrick dates from 1783 when it was instituted by George III to honour distinguished service on the part of Irish peers. The order is no longer in use, but it formerly ranked third in the orders of chivalry after the Orders of the Garter and Thistle, and was the highest honour awarded to Irish peers.

Among Ede and Ravenscroft's records is a specification for the robes of the order. Written by William Webb, it is of interest as it gives details not only of the mantle but also of the under-dress and accessories worn on ceremonial occasions.

For the Knights of Saint Patrick in the year 1809
The Marquis of Ely, Earl O'Neill and Lord Conyngham

Hat	of Blue Sattin with a Band Embroidered Jewel Piece of Blue Sattin with the Star of the Order in the Centre. 3 Feathers Red, Blue and White
Mantle	of Sky Blue Sattin Lined with White Sattin Cordons of Blue and White
Surcoat	the same
The Doublets or Jackets & Breeches	Made of White Sattin Edged with Blue Sattin with Blue Silk and Silver Loops and Buttons Crimson Knee Roses
	Stockings of White Silk White Kid Shoes with Red Roses Badge for Mantle Rosets for Collar White
Sword Belt	Crimson Velvet Scabbard & Belt

The order flourished throughout the 19th century and into the 20th but fell into disuse after Eire became an independent sovereign state. No new knights were appointed and the Most Illustrious Order of Saint Patrick became obsolete on the death of the last remaining knight, the Duke of Windsor, on 28 May 1972.

H.R.H. the Prince of Wales wearing the robes of the Most Honourable Order of the Bath.

74

The Most Honourable Order of the Bath is of ancient origin. Its name is derived from the practice of a knight taking a bath prior to his investiture. This ritual, together with that of spending the night in a solitary vigil of silent prayer, signified the outward and inward cleansing of body and soul, marking a pledge to a future of knightly conduct. These rituals are known to have been practised as early as the 11th century.

The Order of the Bath was revived in 1725 and became the highest military honour during the 18th century, numbering among its knights such eminent leaders as Lord Nelson and the Duke of Wellington. In 1815 a division of the order was created for civil knights. Today, the Order of the Bath has three classes, Knights Grand Cross, Knights Commander, and Companions; in each class there is a military and a civil division.

The mantle of the order is of crimson satin lined with white taffeta and has cordons and tassels of crimson and gold. The order's chapel is the King Henry VII Chapel at Westminster Abbey, where a service of the Most Honourable Order of the Bath is held once every four years.

1818 saw the institution of a new order of chivalry, the Most Distinguished Order of Saint Michael and Saint George. Malta and the Ionian Islands had come under British sovereignty in 1814 and this new order, founded by the Prince Regent on behalf of George III, was to honour the loyalty of outstanding Maltese and Ionian Islanders, as well as to reward British subjects who had rendered distinguished service in the Mediterranean area. Some fifty years later, when the Ionian Islands were ceded to Greece, the Order of Saint Michael and Saint George was restructured, broadening the range of British subjects who were eligible for appointment to it. Appointments to the order are now made to diplomats and other members of the Foreign Office, and to those who have given valuable or loyal service in administration connected with the countries of the Commonwealth or in foreign affairs.

The mantle of the order is of saxon-blue satin lined with scarlet silk and tied with tasselled cordons of blue, scarlet and gold. The chapel of the Order of Saint Michael and Saint George is in St Paul's Cathedral and a service of the order is held there annually.

In the 1860s Queen Victoria instituted two new orders of chivalry specifically associated with the Empire in India. The first, founded on 23 February 1861, was the Most Exalted Order of the Star of India. The mantle of this order was of sky-blue silk lined with white silk, tied with white cordons with tassels of sky-blue and silver. It is of interest to note that the badge and star of this order were, at the time of their introduction, the most costly of the insignia of any of the orders of chivalry, being set with a considerable number of diamonds.

opposite, far left: General Sir John Hackett wearing the mantle and collar of the Most Honourable Order of the Bath (Military Division). The crimson silk satin mantle is fully lined with white silk taffeta. The motto of the order is Tria juncta in uno *(Three joined in one).*

opposite, left: Sir Nicholas Henderson wearing the mantle and collar of the Most Distinguished Order of St Michael and St George. The mantle is of saxon-blue satin, fully lined with scarlet silk. The motto of the order is Auspicium melioris aevi *(Token of a better age).*

Knights Grand Commander of the Exalted Order of the Star of India and of the Most Eminent Order of the Indian Empire attending the coronation of Edward VII in 1902. Both orders are now obsolete.

The second order, founded on 2 August 1886, was the Most Eminent Order of the Indian Empire. The mantle of this order was of a very deep-blue silk lined with white silk, tied with white cordons with tassels of deep-blue and gold. Many of the Indian princes and maharajas were appointed to these orders which were also open to British subjects who had rendered valuable service in connection with the Empire in India.

Ede and Ravenscroft have among their archives details of mantles which were made for knights of these orders, as well as other interesting records such as a letter appointing the firm robemakers to His Highness Sir Bhagvat Sinhji, the Thakore Sahib of Gondal, who was a Knight Grand Commander of the Indian Empire. A number of these Indian dignitaries, wearing mantles of the Indian orders, attended the coronation of Edward VII in 1902.

No appointments have been made to these orders since 1947 and now both the Most Exalted Order of the Star of India and the Most Eminent Order of the Indian Empire are obsolete.

The Royal Victorian Order was instituted by Queen Victoria on 21 April 1896. It was her wish to have an order to which appointments could be made as a personal gift from the sovereign. This continues to be the basis of appointment and consequently this award is particularly highly regarded by those who receive it.

The mantle of the Royal Victorian Order is of dark blue silk edged with scarlet and lined with white silk. It is fastened with tasselled cordons of dark blue and gold. The silks and satins used in the ceremonial dress of all the orders of chivalry are each a unique colour and great care is taken to maintain the correct shade. A recent example of this care occurred in 1985 when Ede and Ravenscroft were asked to make a new mantle for the chancellor of the Royal Victorian Order. This was to be of heavy all-silk satin, in ivory, lined with blue and edged with

Lieutenant Colonel Sir Martin Gilliat wearing the mantle and collar of the Royal Victorian Order. The dark blue satin mantle is edged with scarlet satin and fully lined with white silk. The motto of the order is 'Victoria'.

scarlet silk. The ivory silk satin for this mantle was especially woven and dyed and, consequently, twelve months were required to fulfil the order.

The chapel of the Royal Victorian Order is the Queen's Chapel of the Savoy. This very small private chapel, parts of which date from the 14th century, is the possession of the sovereign as Duke of Lancaster and as such it is outside the authority of the Diocese of London. It has been the chapel of the order since 1937.

In 1986 Ede and Ravenscroft were consulted by the Duchy of Lancaster with regard to the design and material for a hood for the chaplain of the Royal Victorian Order. It is now extremely rare for new items to be designed and added to the dress of any of the orders of chivalry, but after considerable discussion a specification was drawn up and approved by the Duchy of Lancaster:

Chaplain's Hood for the Royal Victorian Order

16″ wide × 18″ deep of Royal Victorian Order blue silk satin interlined and backed with Royal Victorian Order (officers) ivory silk satin. Hand embroidered badge in centre of hood 5″ × 5″ in the form of a Victoria Cross. Border of hood edged with ¼″ Russian braid (no fringe) and 5 gold wire loops, spaced 4″ apart, for attaching to buttons on the cope.

Since Queen Victoria's reign only one new order of chivalry has been established. This is the Most Excellent Order of the British Empire, which was instituted by George V on 17 June 1917 to honour the many people who had contributed so greatly to the war effort but who were not necessarily military personnel. The First World War, unlike previous wars, involved the whole nation and at the time there was no order of chivalry to which civilians could suitably be appointed. This was the major consideration in the founding of the new order. A particular feature of the Order of the British Empire is that it is open equally to men and women. Although the first appointments were made to honour those who had given loyal service to the war effort, George V intended that appointments to this order should be made for a much wider variety of service to the country once the war had ended. This has proved to be the case and the Most Excellent Order of the British Empire is now awarded to many people in all walks of life. It has well been described as the peoples' order of chivalry.

The mantle of this order is of rose-pink satin lined with pearl-grey silk and fastened with cordons of pearl-grey and tassels of rose-pink and silver.

The chapel of the Most Excellent Order of the British Empire, designed in 1957 by the late Lord Mottistone, is in the crypt of St Paul's Cathedral.

Air Chief Marshal Sir John Gingell wearing the mantle and collar of the Most Excellent Order of the British Empire. The rose-pink silk satin mantle is fully lined with pearl grey silk. The motto of the order is 'For God and the Empire'.

Court Dress

Court dress, worn by those attending on the sovereign at Levees and Drawing Rooms, can be said to have had its heyday during Queen Victoria's reign. Regulations were strict and details of required dress were regularly issued by the Lord Chamberlain's Office and printed in the *London Gazette*.

For men, court dress consisted of a black velvet or cloth coat and vest, breeches, silk stockings and buckled shoes. Sword hilts, shoe buckles and buttons were all made of cut steel, but when the Court was in mourning these were replaced with plain black ornaments.

For ladies there were equally detailed regulations, particularly for presentation at Court. The minute attention paid to matters of dress and etiquette can best be appreciated by reading such papers as 'Dress Regulations Approved by the Queen for Her Majesty's Drawing Rooms', published by the Lord Chamberlain in February 1883:

> Ladies attending Her Majesty's Drawing Rooms must appear in full Court Dress with Trains and Plumes according to Regulation.
>
> Feathers must be worn so that they can be clearly seen on approaching Her Majesty, with White Veils or Lappets. Coloured Feathers are inadmissable, but in deep Mourning Black Feathers may be worn.
>
> White Gloves only are to be worn, excepting in case of Mourning, when Black or Grey Gloves are admissable.
>
> High Square-cut Gowns cannot be considered 'Full Dress' and are not admitted at Court. In cases of delicate health Her Majesty is pleased to dispense with the above Regulation.
>
> It is necessary for Ladies who wish to appear in 'High Dress' to obtain Her Majesty's permission through the Lord Chamberlain. This application must always be accompanied by a Medical Certificate.

Equally stringent rules applied to court mourning, described in the following notice in the *London Gazette*:

The Lord Great Chamberlain, the Marquess of Cholmondeley, in levee dress.

Orders for the Court's going into mourning on Wednesday next, the 12th inst., for her late Royal Highness the Duchess d'Alençon, first cousin once removed to Her Majesty the Queen, viz.:— The ladies to wear black dresses, white gloves, black or white shoes, feathers, and fans, pearls, diamonds, or plain gold or silver ornaments. The gentlemen to wear black Court dress, with black swords and buckles. The Court to change the mourning on Wednesday the 19th inst., viz.:— The ladies to wear black dresses, with coloured ribbons, flowers, feathers, and ornaments, or grey or white dresses, with black ribbons, flowers, feathers, and ornaments. The gentlemen to continue the same mourning. And on Saturday, the 22d inst., the Court to go out of mourning.

When Queen Victoria died the Court went into mourning for a full year.

Nowadays, court dress is worn on ceremonial occasions by the Lord Chancellor, the Speaker, High Court judges, and other high-ranking dignitaries of State and Law. This dress, which still consists of black frock coat and vest, breeches, silk stockings and buckled shoes, is worn beneath official robes on occasions such as the Lord Chancellor's Breakfast or the State Opening of Parliament, and some judges and QCs wear the coat and vest beneath their robes on a daily basis.

The following note from the archives was written a century

A levee at St James's Palace in 1910.

84

ago but the regulations for dress vary little from the present day.

Parliament When Opened by The Queen

Lord Chancellor	wears velvet Court suit, Parliamentary robe, gilt buckles, lace bands, frills and ruffles, and full bottom wig.
Peers	wear Parliamentary robe over ordinary morning dress.
Bishops	wear full robes including satin, rochet, sleeves etc. under their Parliamentary robes.
Speaker	wears gold loop gown, full bottom wig over a Court suit, lace frills, ruffles and bands.
Judges	Lord Justices same as Speaker. Common law judges, scarlet robe, hood, mantle, scarf, tippet, bands, girdle, full bottom wig, over a Court suit.

This formal wear has been made by the firm from its earliest days and it continues to supply Court suits for officers of state, judges, and members of staff of the House of Lords and the House of Commons. Outfits are also made for the royal pages along with coatees for the officers of arms. Everyday dress for many of these officers of state and members of the legal profession is the formal suit with black jacket and waistcoat and striped trousers.

Civic and Municipal Robes

Ede and Ravenscroft have by long tradition been robemakers to the Corporation of the City of London (now the Corporation of London), making robes for the Lord Mayor, the sheriffs and aldermen, and the common councillors, and the Lord Mayor's three household officers: the Swordbearer, the Common Cryer and Serjeant-at-Arms, and the City Marshal. The earliest mention of a mayor of London occurs *c.*1189, and the title of Lord Mayor of London is recorded first in 1414, the time of the famous Sir Richard Whittington's mayoralty.

The basic style of the civic robe dates from the 15th century. By that time the City livery companies had, as their name suggests, established the use of gowns by which the wearer could be recognised as belonging to a certain company. Sixteenth-century drawings depicting liverymen show robes which have changed little during the intervening centuries. The livery companies evolved from the medieval craft guilds, and their members laid the foundations of local government as we know it today. Indeed, the Lord Mayor and sheriffs of

opposite: The Lord Mayor of London, Sir Christopher Collett, wearing the scarlet robe. The Lord Mayor's robe is adapted from his alderman's robe by the addition of a train, which is looped over the left arm.

The Lord Mayor of London, preceded by his household officers and followed by the two sheriffs who are candidates for the mayoralty, walks in procession from St Lawrence Jewry to the Guildhall, where the election of the new Lord Mayor is to take place.

London are still elected by the liverymen of the various livery companies.

The Lord Mayor of London has a total of five robes which are worn on appropriate occasions during his term of office. The most familiar is probably the scarlet robe with its sable fur and black velvet trim. This is an alderman's robe to which a train has been added. The robe is worn, among other occasions, in the Lord Mayor's Show each autumn when the new Lord Mayor rides in procession through the streets of the City to the Royal Courts of Justice in the Strand. There he is presented to the Lord Chief Justice and the judges of the Queen's Bench Division in the last of the ceremonies which mark the start of his term of office. The Lord Mayor's violet robe, trimmed with narrow strips of black bear fur, differs from the scarlet robe in colour only. A black and gold robe is worn at various banquets, at certain services at St Paul's Cathedral, and at presentations of the Honorary Freedom of the City.

The crimson velvet reception robe with its ermine cape is worn when the sovereign visits the City and is welcomed at Temple Bar with the traditional ceremony of presentation of the City Sword, as well as at state or royal thanksgiving services at St Paul's Cathedral, and when the head of a foreign state is received at the Guildhall. This robe is very similar to an earl's coronation robe. It is tied with gold tasselled cordons and

Ward beadles are livery company officers whose duties include marshalling the liverymen at the election of the Lord Mayor of London.

left: *The Lord Mayor of London wears the reception robe to greet George V and Queen Mary when they visited the City on the occasion of the King's Silver Jubilee. The dress coat bag on the Lord Mayor's ermine cape was originally worn to protect the robes from the powdered wig.*

below: *The coronation robe worn by the Lord Mayor of London at the coronation of George IV.*

has white satin shoulder bows which hold in place the Lord Mayor's gold collar (or chain) of linked Ss.

Finally there is the magnificent coronation robe. This robe is of crimson velvet lined with white silk and is trimmed on each side, from the front edge to the side seam, with four bars of white miniver fur edged with gold lace.

The sheriffs and aldermen of the Corporation of London each have two robes: one is scarlet and the other violet, both trimmed with fur and velvet. They do not have a train but are otherwise identical to those worn by the Lord Mayor. Common councillors have one robe which is worn on ceremonial occasions. It is made of dark blue silk trimmed with fitch fur.

Despite the richness of the cloth and the gold lace and ornaments involved in the making of many ceremonial robes there is always an element of economy in their use. As we have already seen, new robes are never made unnecessarily and in many cases trimmings and ornaments are re-used. This economy appears once again in the records of civic and municipal robes. As recently as 1982 the Keeper of the Guildhall asked Ede and Ravenscroft to make thirty-two new common councillors' robes. The firm's quotation included the following specification:

Thirty-two robes of dark blue silk made up to the sizes as your old robes, the fitch fur to be used from thirty of your robes and the further two to be made complete using new fur from our stock. The two old robes in question are to be returned to you intact. We wish to advise you that we are having the material woven and fast dyed in the hope that it will hold the shade over the years.

In the same year the firm made a new black and gold robe for the Lord Mayor of London. The old robe was about twenty years old and had definitely seen better days. This robe is of special significance because it was made for Lady Donaldson, the first woman to hold the office of Lord Mayor in the long history of the Corporation of London. This robe was

of lightweight black silk damask, with train, full trimmed on facings, cape collar, hem and train, with 2¼" gold plate lace. Sleeves, side panels and train fully trimmed with hand made gold ornaments and gold embroidered wings on the sleeve heads.

At the proclamation of the accession of George V, the Lord Mayor of London is resplendent in his black and gold gown. The silk tufts on the black gowns of his Swordbearer (left) *and Serjeant-at-Arms are clearly visible.*

Lady Donaldson, being less tall than some of her predecessors, requested that the hem should be unusually deep, to ensure the continued use of this magnificent robe.

The Municipal Corporations Act of 1835 resulted in the establishment of many new mayoralties throughout the British Isles and the Victorian era saw a tremendous increase in demand for the design and supply of new civic robes. These were based on the long-established patterns used by the Corporation of London.

Among its archives Ede and Ravenscroft has a handwritten manual, compiled during the last quarter of the 19th century, in which there is a record of the many new robes designed and made for civic dignitaries of the time. It begins with illustrated descriptions of the scarlet and violet robes worn by officers and members of the Corporation of London, labelled No.1 and No.2, and goes on to list the specifications for the robes of mayors and councillors of no less than three hundred and ninety different boroughs, as well as those for the robes of masters, wardens and clerks of over thirty of the City of London livery companies. Although most of the entries refer to robes No.1 and No.2 for their basic design and colour, there is a

Members of the Watermen's Company compete annually in Doggett's Coat and Badge race, rowed between London Bridge and Cadogan Pier, Chelsea. The prize for the winners of the race, instituted by Thomas Doggett in 1715, is the scarlet coat and silver arm-badge.

The State and Civic Sword Bearer of Carmarthen with the Prince and Princess of Wales. The city's sword is dated 1546, when the office of sword bearer was created by royal warrant.

very wide variety of trimming and decoration, amplified by numerous small sketches. Some entries are very brief, such as that for the Mayor of Bangor, whose robe is 'the same as No.1 but with fitch fur – 17 skins'. Others appear to the lay person to be much abbreviated but no doubt conveyed all the necessary detail to the robemaker. The Head Usher at the Mansion House, for example, wears a robe of 'black queen's cord, QC shape, velvet facings, cape, wings and cuts, back slit not bound, velvet 1½" wide with silk tufts on top of sleeves only'.

A few robes were strikingly different both in colour and design, such as a Caernarvon alderman's robe which is of 'alpaca cord trimmed yellow velvet, something like a London Alderman but with a large Inverness cape'.

We learn, too, that the first Mayor of Richmond wore his London alderman's purple robe for his term of office from 1890–1, but that his successor had a robe made the same as No.1, London scarlet, but of scarlet silk rather than superfine cloth, and with musquash trimmings.

Over the last century many of these new designs have become well established, so that when a new robe is required it is simply a matter of selecting the appropriate ledger and checking the specification with the customer. It would be unusual not to find an entry since, more than fifty years ago, the firm could already claim to have made the robes for twenty-eight London boroughs and a total of three hundred and eighty-five cities and towns throughout the British Isles. They also made and exported robes to the civic dignitaries of overseas cities as far apart as Cape Town and Ottawa.

Clerical Dress

The Victorian era saw a marked increase in the demand for all types of clerical dress. This had always been part of the firm's trade, successive Archbishops of Canterbury and numerous bishops and clergy featuring in the ledgers through the years, but by the mid-19th century Ede & Son were offering a considerably wider range. The examples below from an old brochure of clerical dress give an idea of the range of this section of the business.

opposite: These magnificent copes were worn at the coronation of Edward VII and Queen Alexandra.

This Victorian catalogue is evocative of Trollope's cathedral closes.

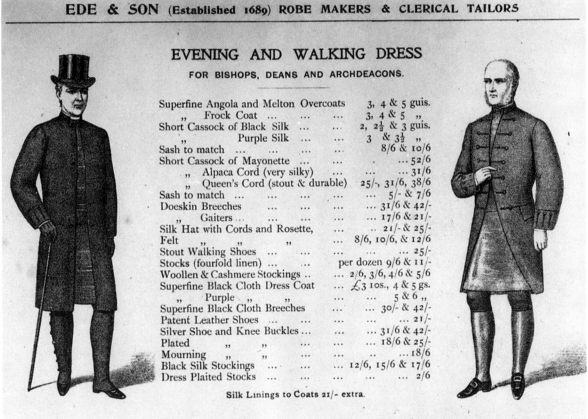

EDE & SON (Established 1689) ROBE MAKERS & CLERICAL TAILORS

EVENING AND WALKING DRESS

FOR BISHOPS, DEANS AND ARCHDEACONS.

Superfine Angola and Melton Overcoats	3, 4 & 5 guis.
„ Frock Coat	3, 4 & 5 „
Short Cassock of Black Silk	2, 2½ & 3 guis.
„ Purple Silk	3 & 3½ „
Sash to match	8/6 & 10/6
Short Cassock of Mayonette	...52/6
„ Alpaca Cord (very silky)	...31/6
„ Queen's Cord (stout & durable)	25/-, 31/6, 38/6
Sash to match	... 5/- & 7/6
Doeskin Breeches	... 31/6 & 42/-
„ Gaiters	... 17/6 & 21/-
Silk Hat with Cords and Rosette, ...	.. 21/- & 25/-
Felt „ „ „ ...	8/6, 10/6, & 12/6
Stout Walking Shoes	... 25/-
Stocks (fourfold linen)	per dozen 9/6 & 11/-
Woollen & Cashmere Stockings	2/6, 3/6, 4/6 & 5/6
Superfine Black Cloth Dress Coat ...	£3 10s., 4 & 5 gs.
„ Purple „ „	5 & 6 „
Superfine Black Cloth Breeches ...	... 30/- & 42/-
Patent Leather Shoes	... 21/-
Silver Shoe and Knee Buckles	... 31/6 & 42/-
Plated „ „ „ ...	... 18/6 & 25/-
Mourning „ „	...18/6
Black Silk Stockings	12/6, 15/6 & 17/6
Dress Plaited Stocks	... 2/6

Silk Linings to Coats 21/- extra.

In submitting the following list of prices, EDE & SON can at the same time guarantee the quality of the cloths, which are selected from the best manufacturers.

EDE & SON devote great care to the cut of the above suit, and their patrons may rely on the strictest attention being paid in every way.

93 & 94, CHANCERY LANE, LONDON.   Telephone 602 HOLBORN.

The Legal Year

The legal year begins in October when the Lord Chancellor's Breakfast takes place at the beginning of the Michaelmas Law Sittings. The Lord Chancellor is perhaps more familiar as the great officer of state who presides over the House of Lords, but he is also head of the judiciary and in this capacity he leads the procession of judges and other legal dignitaries from the House of Lords to Westminster Abbey for the service which marks the start of the Michaelmas Sittings.

This is an occasion when the judiciary appear in full ceremonial dress. The Lord Chancellor, the Master of the Rolls, the Lord Justices of Appeal, and the Presidents of the Probate, Divorce and Admiralty Divisions wear their magnificent black and gold robes. These are of the finest black silk damask, trimmed with 3-inch-wide gold lace and handmade gold ornaments. They are worn with lace bands, stock with lace ends, ruffles, and a full-bottomed wig, over the traditional court dress with gilt-buckled shoes.

At the Lord Chancellor's Breakfast the judges can be seen in their scarlet robes, hood and mantle trimmed with white ermine, which they wear over their court dress of black coat

opposite: The Lord Chancellor, Lord Mackay of Clashfern, wearing full ceremonial dress.

The judges and their chief clerks walk in procession from Westminster Abbey at the beginning of the Michaelmas Law Sittings.

The court coat, with its wide cuffs, and vest can be seen clearly in this 19th-century drawing of a QC.

opposite: Former Master of the Rolls, Lord Denning, in ceremonial dress. The black damask gown is trimmed with handmade gold ornaments and gold plate lace.

and waistcoat, knee breeches, black silk stockings, and shoes with steel buckles. With this ceremonial dress the judges wear full-bottomed wigs.

After the first day of the Michaelmas Sittings the scarlet robe is replaced by a black cloth robe trimmed with white ermine, and this is worn for the remainder of the Michaelmas Sittings and through the Hilary Sittings which commence in January. During the law sittings of Easter and Trinity the judges wear a robe of purple cloth trimmed with silk. With the black and purple robes the smaller tye wig is worn.

The Lord Chief Justice, Lord Lane, in scarlet robe and full-bottomed wig. He is wearing the Lord Chief Justice's collar.

The judges' scarlet robes, with court dress and full-bottomed wigs, are worn on a variety of other occasions, such as in the presence of the sovereign in the House of Lords, at services in St Paul's Cathedral, at the Meeting of Judges in the Old Bailey, and on Red Letter Days. These include Her Majesty the Queen's Birthday, Accession and Coronation Days, Lord Mayor's Day, Ash Wednesday, Ascension Day, and some dozen or more saints' days.

The tradition of judges wearing scarlet robes is of some antiquity and can be traced back at least to the reign of Henry VI in the mid-15th century, a fact established by detailed paintings of the time. By the reign of Charles I the dress of judges and other officers of law was subject to regulation, changing according to the law terms which were based on the Church calendar. James Planché, a 19th-century Somerset

100

A Chief Justice, Lord Justice Mann, in the black and gold robe. Gilt-buckled shoes are part of court dress and are worn on all ceremonial occasions.

Herald, in his *Cyclopaedia of Costume*, published in 1876, quotes an order regarding the dress regulations to be observed by the judges in 1635:

> The judges in term time are to sit at Westminster in their black or violet gowns . . . The facings of their gowns, hoods, and mantles is with changeable taffata, which they must begin to wear upon Ascension Day . . . and continue these robes until the Feast of Simon and Jude; and upon Simon and Jude's day the judges begin to wear their robes faced with white miniver, and so continue that facing till Ascension Day again. Upon all holy days which fall in the term . . . the judges sit in scarlet faced with taffata, when taffata is to be worn, and with furs or miniver when furs and miniver are to be worn. When the judges go to Paul's to the sermon in term, or any other church, they ought to go in scarlet gowns . . .

For over a century Ede and Ravenscroft have supplied a document now entitled 'Judges' Robing List', which clarifies the dress regulations for all the divisions of the judiciary throughout the legal year and on the numerous special days and state occasions. Legal dress is a complicated subject and this list, based on the authority of years of robemaking for the judiciary, has proved invaluable to many. The present list was issued during the reign of George V.

A High Court judge, Mr Justice Drake, in scarlet mantle and hood. He is holding his 'Oxford Gloves'. (On the first visit of a High Court judge to Oxford he is presented with two pairs of gloves. One by the Vice-Chancellor of Oxford University and the second by the Mayor and Civic Authorities.)

opposite: *A circuit judge, Judge Murchie, in the judges' violet robe with lace stock and ruffles.*

Academic Gowns

The making and supplying of academic dress has been a feature of the firm's work since its early days, although two hundred years ago there were only a few universities, including Oxford, Cambridge, St Andrews, and Durham, and ledger entries were infrequent.

The academic trade increased steadily during the early 19th century, when many new universities were founded, not least among them the University of London. By the 1870s the firm was supplying robes and gowns to more than twenty universities throughout Britain, as well as to a number of specialist colleges, among them the College of Physicians in Edinburgh, the College of Organists, the London College of Music, and the Royal School of Mines. At about the same time the firm began to supply gowns and hoods to universities overseas and by 1920 the names of more than a hundred foreign universities in Europe, America, and many other countries worldwide are recorded in the firm's ledgers. The list includes universities scattered as far apart as Ceylon, Khartoum, Geneva, Nepal, Trinidad, Shanghai and Witwatersrand. All were listed in Rosa Ede's manual, which also contained the British universities and colleges, and gave specifications for some five hundred gowns and hoods.

A typical example of academic dress would be the gown, hood and mortar-board of the Oxford or Cambridge Master of Arts degree. These graduates wear plain black gowns with a gathered yoke at the back and with the typical cut-away pattern on the hanging sleeves. This is a distinguishing mark which varies according to the university. The Oxford MA hood, known as the simple shaped hood, is black lined with red, while the Cambridge MA wears a hood of the full shaped type which is black fully lined with white silk. MA graduates of both universities wear the distinctive square mortar-board with tassel, the exception being Oxford women graduates who are traditionally given the option of wearing the Oxford soft hat.

The academic dress of these long-established universities remains among the most striking, particularly for the higher

opposite: H.R.H. the Duke of Edinburgh, Chancellor of the University of Cambridge, at the honorary degree ceremony.

A 19th-century print of Cambridge gowns. The hood of the MA gown (on the right) is longer than is usual today.

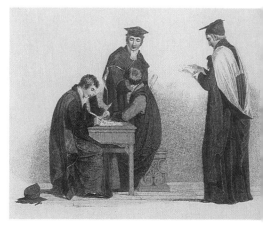

opposite: *A variety of academic gowns, hoods and hats make a colourful sight.*

degrees. An example is the robe for a holder of the degree of Doctor of Divinity. At Oxford this is a bright scarlet gown with starkly contrasting wide black sleeves, a scarlet hood lined with black, and a flat black velvet hat. The Cambridge DD wears a similar scarlet gown with a scarlet hood lined with pink silk, and a flat black velvet hat with gold cord and tassels. A Cambridge Doctor of Law also wears this rather unusual combination of scarlet and pink in a scarlet gown that has wide sleeves which taper to a point level with the hem and which are lined with the same pink silk as the hood and the wide facings down each side of the front. Perhaps most spectacular of all is the robe of the Oxford Doctor of Music. This gown, worn with the same flat black velvet hat as the others, is of ivory flowered silk damask and has wide sleeves, front facings and hood of bright cerise pink.

In most cases the academic dress of a university follows a similar formula. Gowns are usually of one colour but may vary in style according to whether they are for a bachelor's or master's degree or for a doctorate. However, there are exceptions where the doctor's gown differs in colour from that of a bachelor or master. Hoods come in a wide variety of colours and although a university may restrict itself to a fairly small colour range, each degree usually has its individual hood. The exception is when the hood is the same for all faculties as, for example, at the universities of Bristol and Reading.

Hats, too, vary considerably in their design, from the familiar mortar-board to the square soft velvet hat (the 'John Knox'), the round flat velvet hat with its cord and tassels, and many more.

The Encaenia procession in Oxford: the red gowns and Tudor bonnets are worn by Doctors of Civic Law or Medicine, and the gowns with grey facings by Doctors of Letters or Science.

The gowns of the University of Kent were designed by Ede and Ravenscroft. The amount of gold embroidery and lace is an indication of rank. The scarlet gowns are worn by recipients of honorary degrees. (left to right) *Dr J.A. Lawton, Lord Grimond, Professor Bernard Benjamin, Professor John Pirt, Dr D.J.E. Ingram, and Dr V.H.B. Alexander.*

The same style would usually be adopted throughout a university with any exceptions being for doctorates.

The robes and hats of university chancellors, vice-chancellors, provosts and registrars are often more elaborate, being made of damask with varying amounts of gold lace and ornaments. For example, the robe which the Princess Royal wears as Chancellor of the University of London is of black silk damask heavily trimmed with gold lace and ornaments, and her black velvet mortar-board is trimmed with gold lace and a gold bullion tassel.

The mid-1960s saw another surge in the demand for academic dress with the foundation of a number of new universities, such as Aston, Bath, Brunel, Essex and Kent. New academic dress was required by all these establishments and the firm designed many complete sets from chancellor down to holders of first degrees. This gave a certain amount of scope for innovation, particularly where colour was concerned. The splendid new gowns and mortar-boards designed for the chancellor and officers of the University of Essex, for example, are a bright scarlet embellished with wide bands of gold and lace.

At this time many of the newly independent African

countries, especially those in West Africa, were founding their own universities and colleges of higher education. The firm was appointed as official robemakers to a number of these establishments, resulting in the design of new academic dress which reflected the ethnic designs of the countries concerned and gave scope for the imaginative use of colour. In some cases climate was a deciding factor in the choice of design and materials, to ensure that gowns would be suitable for use in the tropics. The traditional lines of the African robe were incorporated in some designs, such as those for Bayero University in Nigeria, while others followed the more traditional European shape. Ibadan University, also in Nigeria, received a splendid range in navy blue damask with long tapering sleeves lined with lime green silk. The decoration was of gold or silver according to rank and the various officers were distinguished by badges depicting their positions within the university.

Ede & Ravenscroft are now the leaders in the field of academic dress, hiring out gowns, hoods and hats to thousands of new graduates for the annual degree ceremonies, and making robes for the chancellors and officers of the majority of British universities and many polytechnics.

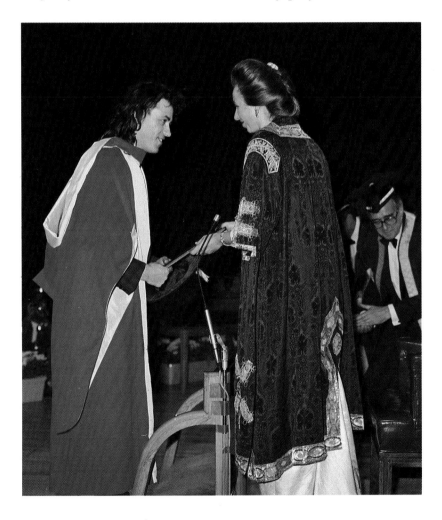

Bob Geldof receives an honorary degree from H.R.H. the Princess Royal, Chancellor of the University of London.

As Ede and Ravenscroft enter their fourth century of robemaking,
their staff continue to uphold the high standards of work
with which the firm has always been associated.
In the workrooms, traditional specialist skills are still in daily use,
ensuring the continuity of robemaking traditions from the past
for the enjoyment of many generations to come.

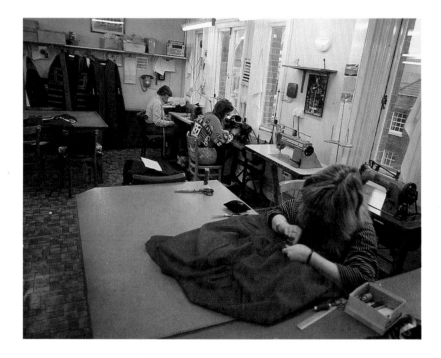

Index

Photographic credits

Butterworth & Co 99; Camera Press 43 (photo: ILN), 44 (photo: Cecil Beaton), 47 (photo: Norman Parkinson), 54 (photo: Peter Abbey), 75 (photo: Jim Bennett); Corporation of London 88 (photo: Clive Totman); Peter Dale 22, 36, 37, 38, 41, 49, 61, 78, 89 (below), 90, 94; Keith Ellis 59, 63, 65, 70 (both), 87; Fleet Group plc 1, 10, 11, 13, 29, 31, 57, 58, 76 (both) 81, 103, 110; J.R. Freeman Ltd 12, 26, 32, 40, 42, 50, 66, 72 (all), 73 (all), 105; Essex County Council 19; Tim Graham 93; A. Grimes 69; Robert Harding Picture Library 20 (Pinacoteca Vaticana), 89 (above); Lord Lichfield 48, 51, 60; By kind permission of the President & Fellows of Magdalen College, Oxford 25; Norman S. Mason-Smith photographer 104; Nick Meers 106, 107; National Geographic Magazine 2; National Portrait Gallery 14, 16, 17, 34, 39, 98; Godfrey New 35, 63, 95; Photolab (photo: Ian Coates) 108, 109; Pitkin Pictorials (photo: Lord Lichfield) 6; The Royal Collection 84–5; Tom Scott Roxburgh LMPA, OMLJ 64; Brian Shuel 91; Spectrum Colour Library 97; Loisjoy Thurstun 86, 102; Universal Pictorial Press 53.